Risk Management of Machinery and Work Equipment

Risk Management of Machinery and Work Equipment

John Glover

First published in the UK in 2010
by

British Standards Institution
389 Chiswick High Road
London W4 4AL

Typeset in Frutiger by Helius – www.helius.biz
Printed in Great Britain by Berforts Group. www.berforts.com

British Library Cataloguing in Publication Data
A catalogue record for this book is available from the British Library

ISBN 978-0-580-67515-7

Biography

John Glover, a graduate of the Institution of Occupational Safety and Health, has practised health and safety law and safety of machinery for a number of years. He has extensive knowledge of the subject and has had published several magazine articles on health and safety practice.

After having worked for a world-leading health and safety organization specializing in machinery safety, John set up his own health and safety consultancy, Glover Associates & Consulting Ltd. This continues to fulfil his vision for the provision of machinery safety and occupational safety services to commerce and industry alike, including energy and power generation.

www.gloverassociates.co.uk

Introduction

Health and safety at work is becoming increasingly significant with the implementation of the Corporate Manslaughter and Homicide Act 2007. Numerous Directives are also being issued by Brussels and implemented into European law across the member states of the European Union.

Successive high-profile accidents have led to renewed calls for changes in the law, following failed prosecutions against large companies and against individuals for manslaughter. The Corporate Manslaughter and Homicide Act makes it easier to convict organizations whose senior managers have breached their duty of care, causing death. Previously, prosecutions have failed against all but the smallest companies, so the Act could potentially see a dramatic rise in the number of corporate manslaughter cases against businesses of all sizes.

This book gives some much-needed guidance and highlights some of the most frequently asked questions on machinery safety and work equipment. However, there are some other key areas that need consideration, and so this book also covers the field of corporate risk management.

An incident that happened back in 1972, when my grandfather was killed in a mining accident due to the lack or failure of a simple system to isolate a piece of machinery, may have sown the seeds for this book. In 2009 the same mistakes are still being made, despite all the legislation and guidance (and improvements) now in place.

While there *is* now more of a focus on effective management and strong leadership in health and safety, there is still a need to make machinery safety simpler and more accessible. Businesses still have difficulty in relating to the legislation, and often perceive it as overwhelming in volume and content.

It is time to cut through the health and safety myths with this reference book, which has been written in a simple, no-nonsense, question and answer style that will be of benefit to engineers, specialists, generalists and line managers alike, and in particular to anyone who is:

- in a health and safety position in the public or private sectors and is about to take responsibilities, or wishes to develop an understanding of the issues relating to machinery safety;
- a full-time or part-time student at undergraduate or postgraduate level in a health and safety subject, who wishes to learn more about machinery safety;
- working as a health and safety consultant, as a lecturer, or as an employee responsible for carrying out training courses in machinery safety for their own employees or clients;
- an engineer or manager responsible for machinery and work equipment as an integral asset of their organization.

I hope you will find long-lasting value from the information contained within this book, and that it will contribute to saving lives.

John Glover

Contents

1   Corporate risk management

1 What is corporate risk management?

Corporate risk management can be defined as 'effectively managing all situations and circumstances that have the potential to affect the corporate body'. By implementing risk management we are complying with our statutory duty of care towards employees and others. It provides a proactive method for identifying, measuring, controlling and financing risk in order to protect the corporation's assets, which can be defined as people and property.

2 What could risk management do for my business?

There would be a systematic shift from constant 'fire-fighting' and 'crisis management' to proactive decision making before any problems arise. Anticipating what might go wrong will become part of everyday business for you, and the management of risks will become an integral part of a risk management system.

3 What is a risk management system?

A risk management system is a set of elements within an organisation's management system exclusively concerned with managing all kinds of risk to the business.

4 What are the consequences of not implementing a risk management system?

Without a risk management system, management will not have an insight into what could go wrong: therefore, they will expend resources addressing problems that could have been identified sooner or avoided altogether. Bear in mind that some problems can be catastrophic and occur without warning; naturally, this can affect the long-term survival of the business, and can mean that the business is, in effect, in constant crisis.

At one end of the scale, the lack of a risk management system could mean a simple failure to meet statutory and duty holder obligations in respect of risk during a project. It may, alternatively, mean a risk of damage or loss to plant and equipment and other assets, resulting in financial loss. Ultimately, the lack of a risk management system could mean risks to the safety of individuals.

It is management's responsibility to reduce future uncertainty.

5 So, can I guarantee success by implementing risk management?

Risk management is no 'magic bullet' or guarantee of success, but it can improve decision making, help avoid unpleasant surprises and improve an organization's chances of success. It will also assist you in increasing your bottom line (i.e. net profits). It has been long recognized that proactive risk management increases an organization's chances of flourishing and economic success. The principle behind it is to think laterally and consider the breadth and diversity of the risks to the organization. Remember that if someone is injured then this could result in a claim for damages and a criminal prosecution, and this could cost a considerable amount of money to defend. The costs would need to be paid out of company profits!

6 What is the most important asset to any organization?

The most valuable asset that any organization has is the talent of its workforce. After all, it is the people that produce the goods and services that allow the organization to profit from its revenues. Even leaving aside the statutory duties, it is just sheer common and business sense to protect such assets.

7 Is there some terminology that we need to understand?

Absolutely. Although it is important that we don't get bogged down in jargon, the following terms cover the essentials.

Accidents are unplanned, uncontrolled events which lead to, or could have led to, loss.

Pure risks are risks which can only result in a 'loss' or 'no loss' outcome; e.g. you have an accident or don't have an accident.

Fundamental risks are indiscriminate and can affect lots of people: a war, shortage of raw material, shortage of labour, etc.

Speculative risks can result in a financial gain or loss, e.g. people either buy your product or not.

Particular risks are particular to that organization, e.g. a company has a fire or has been victim to theft or fraud.

Corporate risks are risks that can adversely affect the corporate body. They can be simply divided into two groups:

- **Internal risks**, which reflect the way in which the organization is managed and what policies and procedures are implemented. These are risks that are within the control of the organization – or should be! Examples of internal risks could be management expertise, financial control, planning, human resources, contractual controls, motivation of the workforce, catastrophe planning and insurance cover.

- **External risks**, which arise from the economic, social or political environment and are effectively beyond the control of the organization. Some examples here could include changes in legislation, economic recession, actions of competitors, environmental issues.

Statutory risks are risks that are controlled by health and safety legislation and could adversely affect the health, safety and welfare of people without necessarily affecting the organization as a whole in the short term. Statutory risks could consist of short-term and long-term physical injury or health effects.

Certain other legal requirements, such as those Acts and regulations associated with fire, explosive atmospheres and environmental issues, should come under the remit of the risk manager and insurers.

Remember that a high incidence of statutory risk can subsequently represent a major corporate risk, and can be very expensive indeed to any organization – we will concentrate on some of the key areas in the next chapters of this book. Indeed, some companies that have operated on a 'fire-fighting' or reactive basis through the years have lost lots of money and backing from various external resources such as insurance companies and investors.

8 Should I employ a risk manager?

That depends on the size and scope of your organization, but you would do well to remember that every aspect of how an organization does business involves risk. Every financial transaction, every product or service delivered and every person employed represents a potential risk of some kind. Some insurance and risk consultants offer specialist advice in areas such a property risk, employment risk, business continuity and occupational health and safety. The floods in southern England during the summer of 2007, as well as some terrorist attacks (that are, thankfully, rare), highlighted the importance of business continuity management. The Association of British Insurers estimated that the total bill for the June and July floods was £3 billion. Specialist consultants can help with a detailed disaster recovery plan to enable your business to trade as quickly and as profitably as possible after such an event.

9 Should we have a risk management policy as well a safety policy?

You could either have separate policies or an integral policy, but risk management is a continually developing process which runs right through an organization's strategy. It should address all risks – past, present and future – to the organization, and these risks must be identified, measured and controlled. In some organizations the risk management plan will need to address constantly changing types and levels of risk – 'dynamic' change.

10 What do you mean by 'dynamic' change?

Take the example of a construction or renovation project: the fire risk here will be much greater than when the building is eventually occupied. This is owing to the constantly changing conditions on site during the different phases of the construction project, and the comings and goings of different contractors. Contractors all come from different working cultures and the different phases of a project each present unique risks, e.g. there may be a risk with large items of plant and machinery coming on or off site; alternatively, it could be a contractor constructing or dismantling large scaffold structures. A risk management plan, in this example, will take into account the continually evolving variety of risks presented by each new phase of the project.

It is worth including here a note on fire regulations for construction sites. There have been an unacceptable number of fire loss events in construction over the last few years, and the industry has had to seriously address exposure to fire. As a result the Construction Confederation, the Loss Prevention Council and insurance companies have got together and developed a code of practice related to fire prevention for construction sites. This is being policed by the insurance industry, but they tend to focus on the major projects as they have only a limited number of personnel to monitor compliance with the code. This means that, where the code is concerned, the small-to-medium-size sector is left to self-regulate.

If you think about it for a minute, the lower end of the construction industry sector operates on tighter margins and fewer resources; therefore, companies that fail to implement risk management procedures could easily find themselves exposed to a major fire risk in buildings under construction. In addition to this is the fact that many small sub-contractors employ itinerant operators and workers without any formal training. The language barrier is a significant factor in the construction industry, particularly with the free movement of workers within the EU, and care must be taken to provide adequate instruction or training to workers with little or no English language skills. If a fire occurs then the principle contractor would be involved in a complex legal wrangle, with the possibility of a loss of future business and even losing insurance cover! As well as penalty charges for delays in completing the project, there are the additional breaches of the law to consider, and how the bad publicity would affect any future tenders.

11 Is there an explicit requirement in legislation to implement risk management?

Yes. Under the Management of Health and Safety at Work Regulations 1999: Regulation 3, there is an explicit requirement for an organization to carry out a risk assessment and, if employing five or more people, to record the details; there is more about this in subsequent chapters. The essence of good management is also set out in Regulation 5 of the above, for health and safety arrangements to be integrated with management. The four elements it outlines are:

- planning,
- organizing,
- control,
- monitoring and review.

Although this is directed at health and safety, these elements could equally apply to any other aspect of the business, e.g. employing people, ordering goods, using sub-contractors and organizing training for employees. It is good practice to identify with the above and most organizations are now beginning to demonstrate this by getting certification to BS OHSAS 18001, *Occupational health and safety management systems – Requirements*, which is an occupational health and safety management system specification.

Essentially, the implementation of BS OHSAS 18001 helps in a variety of respects: minimizing risk to employees, improving an existing occupational health and safety management system, demonstrating diligence, gaining assurance, etc. The benefits of compliance can be substantial.

2 Risk manager *vs* insurance manager

1 What is the role of insurance in risk management?

Most safety practitioners would probably argue that insurance is a poor tool of risk management, as insurers are very selective nowadays and only take on good business risks. Today's risk environment is changing and evolving more rapidly than ever before, and it has been suggested that underwriting should factor in climate change scenarios, terrorism and disaster planning into premiums, rather than simply basing decisions on historical records. A good risk manager should be well aware of the climate of change among the large insurers.

While management should not expose the organization to any excessive risk, some risks may be uninsurable or very expensive to insure against. It is important not only to identify risks, but also to quantify the financial loss of not controlling them – so, when considering insurance, be guided by the extent of loss incurred should a particular event occur, and not just by the probability of it occurring. The factor that you can really influence to an acceptable level by good risk management techniques is the probability of *loss* occurring.

Insurance can be expensive, but is not to be ignored as it can form part of a risk management policy.

2 But do risk managers attend to the company's insurance needs?

Yes, of course they do. However, they know that external insurance protection may not be the most economical and beneficial way of protecting against various risks. He or she knows that prevention or control of loss should always be the first consideration in dealing with risk. For example, during the floods in southern England in the summer of 2007 some businesses came to a standstill, and lost a considerable amount of revenue – some of which may never be regained – as there were no contingency plans. Other companies had planned for a possible disaster and protected their assets, such as people, finances, materials and equipment. They were able to anticipate the likely effects and took measures to reduce the likely impact, such as transferring production elsewhere and having computer records stored with a third party.

A risk manager will only transfer some of the risk via insurance, as insurers may or may not pay out in certain circumstances, such as natural disasters.

3 What is the difference between the insurance manager and a risk manager?

They may be accommodated in the same department, but their functions are different. An insurance manager's role is to find the best terms and conditions for insurance at the lowest possible costs. He or she may not consider all of the risks that have to be controlled by statute if they don't consider them to be significant in terms of direct losses. Some of them simply go to an insurance broker and place their order via them. Remember that insurance brokers are paid commission based on insurance fees paid to the insurers by the insured. As premiums rise then so does commission, so a lot here depends on the integrity of the insurance broker.

The risk manager's role is to find the most cost-effective way to control risks, and insurance is viewed as a last resort after all other means have been exhausted. Generally, the risk manager would implement the company's safety policy into the risk management policy. The aim of the safety policy is to ensure that the organization's activities do not impinge upon the wellbeing of people, whilst the risk management policy is to ensure that the management strategies will control all risks that could impinge upon the wellbeing of the organization.

A good policy will look after employees, service users and customers, and also look at trends in, for example, the commodities and financial markets, customer actions and consumer taste.

4 Why does a broker charge a fee when they already receive commission from the insurer?

The commission received by the broker from an insurer is to cover the initial expense involved in setting up the policy. The broker fee is an administration charge that is calculated on the ongoing management and service required for an account. This would include at least the general service provided by the account manager and support staff through the year, including the renewal process, and claims management.

5 What does a professional indemnity insurance policy cover?

A professional indemnity (PI) insurance policy protects an organization against legal liability for claims arising out of advice or services provided to clients for a fee or for some other benefit (e.g. commission). PI policies cover claims made under common law (negligence) and for breach of statutes which govern a professional's activities – such as the Health and Safety at Work etc. Act 1974.

6 Will a PI policy cover an organization for the actions of consultants, sub-contractors or agents who provide advice or services on their behalf?

Yes, a PI policy will cover a person for their liability arising out of acts, errors or omissions committed by a consultant, sub-contractor or agent who provides advice or services on their behalf. Generally, a PI policy will not cover the liability of the consultant, sub-contractor or agent, who will be expected to hold his or her own PI policy. So, for example, if a company sub-contracts a consultant to carry out a risk assessment document for their client, and then delivers this document to the client on the company's own headed notepaper, then the company would do well to get PI cover as they will assume some liability.

7 How does an insurance company work out the cost of insurance?

Insurance companies use probability theory in calculating premiums, and one of the methods in general use is:

Premium $= (P \times C) + E$

Where:

P = Probability of the loss occurring
C = Average size of loss that occurs
E = Loading for expenses and profit

The values for P and C will depend on the nature of the organization's activities, the type of management practices used, previous claims, etc, and these factors can dramatically affect the final premium. Nowhere is this more apparent than with car insurance: as an example, for comparison only, these are the differences in annual premium between two people who want similar cover:

17-year-old male: £2,906.25

55-year-old female: £257.65

This is an extreme example, but it illustrates the cost of risk. A young male driver is statistically much more likely than a middle-aged female to be involved in an accident, and therefore represents a greater risk to the insurance company: this is reflected in his paying a premium ten times greater than that of his female counterpart! The same principle applies in industry and business, whether it be a factory or processing plant with large items of plant and machinery, an office, or whatever you care to mention.

8 What is meant by the legal term 'negligence', in the context of risk management?

In law, negligence consists of doing something that a person of ordinary prudence would not do under the same or similar circumstances, or failing to do something that a person of ordinary prudence would do under the same or similar circumstances. This can take the form of, for example, negligence in:

- drawing up or reviewing plans for a product;
- maintaining the machines that make the component parts of the product;
- anticipating probable uses of the product;
- inspecting or testing the product adequately;
- issuing warnings or instructions, or inadequate warnings or instructions;
- releasing the product into the stream of commerce;
- any other aspect of the manufacturing or distribution process where due care is not used.

Negligence cases involve all types of accidents. Common accidents involving negligence include slip and fall accidents, trip and fall accidents, store accidents, accidents at home or a friend's home. Using a defective product or piece of machinery falls under the 'negligence' heading.

Accidents and injuries at work are often caused by defective or faulty work equipment. The Provision and Use of Work Equipment Regulations 1998 (PUWER 98) apply to all work equipment. 'Work equipment' can be found in almost all work locations, including many places of public interest such as retail outlets, libraries and museums, and is defined as meaning 'any machinery, appliance, apparatus, tool or installation for use at work (whether exclusively or not)'. 'Use' in relation to work equipment means 'any activity involving work equipment and includes starting, stopping, programming, setting, transporting, repairing, modifying, maintaining, servicing and cleaning'.

Case study

A UK-based company found itself at risk of negligence claims when an external audit highlighted that some employees were working with poorly maintained machinery. The company decided to 'risk manage' the situation by investing in some of their engineers attending risk management courses on work equipment. This gave the engineers a much greater understanding of their duties under both statutory and civil law, and an understanding of 'negligence' in relation to their roles. It also gave the company a better spread of risk, with some being transferred via insurance and an element being managed in-house.

Following the training course investment the company implemented a much more rigorous maintenance procedure, as the external audit had found that they had been falling short of Regulation 5 of the Provision and Use of Work Equipment Regulations 1998, i.e. 'maintenance with no detailed logs in existence'. A maintenance log is required under the regulations for high-risk equipment, and was necessary in this case. A detailed maintenance log was then introduced in both electronic and hard formats, which was found to be logical, reasonable and defendable whilst reducing the business's exposure to risk.

If the company had not taken this course of action they would have been at risk of breaching health and safety legislation, and a possible future civil claim.

. . . .

3   Health and safety and the law

1 What is health and safety at work all about?

It is about keeping employees and others that could be affected by the conduct of your undertaking safe and free from ill health, injury, damage or loss.

People were forced to work in unsafe environments during the Industrial Revolution, and a large increase in deaths, serious injuries and severe health problems brought a realization among some people in authority that controls at work were necessary. In more recent times an unacceptable rate of workplace fatality, injury and ill health led to a revision of health and safety in the UK by the Robins Committee in 1972, which led to the Health and Safety at Work etc. Act 1974.

Employers have a legal duty to ensure the health, safety and welfare of employees and others while they are at work or as a 'conduct of their undertaking'.

2 What do you mean 'conduct of their undertaking'?

In general terms a work activity is an active term to describe something that is actually taking place involving workers, processes and so on. An example in public safety terms could be the risks to the public posed by the activities of a construction site – for example, scaffolding could fall on passers by – whereas the 'conduct of an undertaking' is a more passive concept. A duty holder could exist where no actual work activity is carried out, for example a public authority play park, where the undertaking of the authority is the provision of play equipment to the public. The duty holder has a duty to make sure that the risks relating to the play park and equipment are controlled.

3 But is all this legislation fairly new and complicated?

No, quite the opposite in fact! The first piece of modern legislation on working conditions was the Factory Health and Morals Act way back in 1802, which had very modest aims but was introduced on the back of the Industrial Revolution, when mill and factory owners put orphan children to work in terrible conditions. These children had no means of redress and many died or suffered from lifelong injuries and health problems. Similar situations still exist in the poorer parts of the world today, and there are in excess of 200m children in the world under the age of 14 years currently being exploited and obliged to carry out the most demoralizing and dangerous tasks.

4 Is it just the employers that have duties?

The employers certainly have the major responsibility for ensuring that standards of health and safety are maintained, but there are other people that have responsibilities and this is a point that some people miss to their peril! For example the self-employed, people in control of premises, building and property owners, and even employees have legal responsibility for health and safety compliance in addition to the employer.

5 Can you briefly describe the rise of health and safety?

The emphasis here should really be on the more recent developments that have taken place since the 1970s. With ever-changing technology, work activities have become more complex and the severity of the risks to health and safety has increased. There are many more toxic substances, bigger buildings, more crowded trains, etc; this has resulted in a rise in associated risks to workers, and a reactive approach was unacceptable. In the 1960s there was also a lack of protection for members of the public and the self-employed, so a more proactive approach was necessary.

This led to the Health and Safety at Work etc. Act 1974, which meant that for the first time every employer, self-employed person and employee had duties and responsibilities. The Act forced people to become proactive in managing risks covering all work activities, regardless of occupation.

6 How much of an influence is the European Union on UK legislation?

The EU is the single greatest influence on the development of legislation in the UK. If the member states don't implement European policy then they can be punished within the European courts. Article 100a of the Treaty of Rome provides for the bulk of Directives on health and safety. This places obligations on EU member states to implement secondary legislation, such as regulations or Directives that have been issued as a result of primary European legislation that all members are bound by, i.e. the Treaty of Rome. When the Council of Ministers issues Directives, member states must amend their law and incorporate the provisions of the Directive.

7 Can you explain a bit about common law?

Sometimes this can confuse people, but it really is quite simple. The legislative instrument of the state formally passes statutory law, which is a source of both criminal and common law. This means that the

UK Parliament has written down and codified the law in Acts and regulations. For example, the Health and Safety at Work etc. Act 1974 is statutory law (and entirely criminal law), and contains duty of care obligations placed on employers that are to be discharged to employees or a third party. These Acts are explicit statements of what the duty is, whereas common law duties are closer to principles of care and are subject to interpretation or argument, as common law is an unwritten and essentially judge-made law, laid down in court decisions and found in law reports.

The 'duty of care' under common law effectively obliges an individual to take reasonable care to avoid acts or omissions which they can reasonably foresee are likely to injure their neighbour or anyone else. Employers owe a duty of a care to their employees, contractors, visitors and members of the public, as well as others.

8 What is the difference between civil law and criminal law?

Common law and statutory law are applied within the criminal court structures. Civil law and criminal law are distinct and use different court structures and procedures when processing the law. Civil law regulates the rights, duties and obligations arising from transactions or disputes between individuals or the state. This may involve one party having to compensate another, and an example could be an employee or member of the public suing an organization for damage or loss. An organization should have employers' liability insurance as a legal requirement and display the certificate at work. An employer could claim protection under this insurance, but they will not necessarily be successful. The insurance company would investigate the claim, and then advise whether settlement of the claim is justified or not. Any non-settlement would mean that the plaintiff would proceed to the civil courts for a hearing. This is why you read about these major cases regularly in the press: even if the company is willing to settle out of court, the insurance company may not be.

Criminal law is non-insurable and is only concerned with conduct which the state has decided ought to be repressed and punished by some sanction or penalty, such as a fine or imprisonment. This means in plain English that if an organization is in breach of the Health and Safety at Work etc. Act 1974 then they would be subject to a fine (non-insurable) under criminal law, and could be subject to claims for compensation under civil law.

9 Should you keep previous employers' liability insurance certificates?

Until October 2008, insurance certificates were to be kept for 40 years after the expiry date because claims for industrial diseases are often made many years after the disease is caused. For example, asbestosis can take 10 to 20 years for it to become life threatening, and knowing the insurance details of the employer 20 years ago is vital in compensation claims. However, this was changed in 2008 and there is now no need to keep certificates; but this has only highlighted the need to keep detailed management systems in place.

10 What if the employer doesn't have employers' liability insurance?

In general you need employers' liability insurance if you have people working for you.

The Health and Safety Executive enforces the law, along with local authorities, and if an employer does not have a certificate that shows a minimum insurance cover for £5 million then they can be fined up to

£2,500 for each and every day they trade without suitable cover. Failure to display a certificate (or provide access to an electronic copy) can result in a £1,000 fine.

11 As an employer, what am I responsible for in respect of health and safety law?

You are responsible for the health, safety and welfare of your employees whilst at work – and while they are away from work too, remember, if they are working at another site. You are also responsible for the health, safety and welfare of people who may resort to your premises, e.g. visitors, customers, contractors, tradesmen, delivery drivers, passers-by and even thieves!

The duties and responsibilities include:

- providing a safe place of work;
- maintaining the place of work in a safe condition;
- providing a safe means of access to and egress from the place of work;
- maintaining plant and equipment in a safe condition;
- preventing exposure of your employees and others to unacceptable hazards that could cause injury or ill health;
- ensuring that employees follow a safe system of work;
- ensuring that employees receive information, instruction, training and supervision, including foreign workers with little or no understanding of English;
- ensuring that you prepare a written health and safety policy if you have five or more employees;
- carrying out a risk assessment of work activities and recording the significant findings if you have five or more employees;
- carrying out assessments in respect of the use and storage of hazardous, dangerous and explosive substances;

- carrying out fire risk assessments;
- using and consulting with competent persons in respect of health and safety;
- preparing emergency plans and procedures;
- consulting with and informing your staff of risks and control measures.

It is also worth remembering that under Section 3 of the Health and Safety at Work etc. Act 1974, there does not need to be actual harm to the third parties to be in breach. It is enough for them to be 'at risk' of exposure. So, for example, if you had some contractors working on your site doing some maintenance activities and they were potentially exposed to moving parts of an unguarded machine, or even a by-product such as certain types of dust, then you would be in breach of the law. Numerous businesses miss this very point!

12 Who has ultimate responsibility for health and safety in an organization?

A company is a legal entity and should be thought of as a 'person'. If the company were to commit a health and safety offence then it is the company that is charged with the offence. However, the company has specified positions with people to fill them under company law, and it is they who would represent the company in all matters. All limited companies must have at least one secretary and one director. Should the company be in breach of health and safety law, the directors would represent the company in court.

It is worth bearing in mind that the Health and Safety Executive (HSE) has issued a guidance note on company directors' responsibilities for health and safety, which clearly sets out what is expected of company directors in undertaking their responsibilities for health and safety within their company. It is possible that at some time in the future there could be regulations for directors' duties.

13 What are the directors' duties?

The directors collectively represent the company and, under Section 37 of the Health and Safety at Work etc. Act 1974, a director, company secretary or holder of another senior management position could be personally prosecuted if they consented to the commission of an offence or acted with neglect in respect of that offence.

The corporate body could also be prosecuted for the offence in addition to an individual if they were also responsible. There is an HSE guidance document on directors' responsibilities that lists five action points that they should follow for them to successfully discharge their responsibilities.

If no board director wants to take on health and safety responsibilities then the chief executive will assume overall responsibility; however, all directors have a 'collective responsibility'.

14 What happens if one of our employees causes an accident, which results in injury to themselves or another person?

An employer is responsible for the wrongful acts of their employees if those acts are committed during the course of their employment. This is known as 'vicarious liability', which arises from a contractual relationship between the parties, and one person is held responsible for the actions of another.

15 What is a health and safety policy, and do we really need one?

Under the Health and Safety at Work etc. Act 1974, an employer must produce a written health and safety policy if they employ five or more people. Employees must be aware of the safety policy and should be given information, instruction and training in its content, use and their own responsibilities. Employees should either be given a copy of the policy or it could be displayed in a prominent position in the workplace. It should also be seen as a 'working document' and be reviewed regularly by the employer and kept up to date.

16 What if we don't have one?

Then that is a criminal offence I'm afraid. If there is an accident at your place of work then an investigating officer of the HSE is likely to ask to see your safety policy, as well as risk assessment records and training records. There have been prosecutions for failing to have a safety policy, and for having a totally inadequate one, too! The safety policy should be seen as a communications tool between the employer and the workforce, as it is their reference guide on how to perform tasks safely. It will detail who has risk assessment responsibility for each department, control measures as a result of assessments, and where they can be found, etc.

17 What is negligence?

Many civil claims of damages are based on negligence, with the claimant alleging that he or she has suffered injury as a result of the defendant's negligence.

In order to establish negligence the following questions must be answered:

- Did the defendant owe a duty of care to the claimant?
- Was there a breach of that duty?
- Is there proof of negligence, i.e. were the damages or losses as a direct result of the breach of duty?

The existence of a duty situation between employer and employee has long been recognized, and most cases turn on the second point, i.e. was the employer negligent? The duty is determined by the employee contract.

18 How can an employer defend a claim?

Only one action can be brought against an employer in respect of injuries that arise out of one incident. A claimant can bring an action against an employer under two different headings: a breach of statutory duty, or a breach of the duty owed by the employer to the employee at common law. A claim can be presented under the two headings simultaneously, but if the employee wins then only one set of damages is awarded. However, the defendant would need to defend against each heading where liability is claimed.

The defendant may be able to satisfy the court that he or she owed no duty of care towards the defendant or that he or she wasn't negligent. An employer won't be held liable for an injury if they did not owe a duty of care. They may also be able to show that the injury was the sole fault of the employee, as the employee cannot put the employer in breach intentionally. The proviso here is that the employer has done everything that statutory law has asked of him. There is also the defence of contributory negligence, where an employer could argue that although they were negligent the employee failed to take sufficient care for his or her own safety, and as such the court may reduce the damages to reflect this.

There is also a time limit set down for someone to pursue a claim. If the issue is injury or death then the time limit is three years, after which the right to sue for compensation disappears. In some circumstances (such as ill health) then the limitation is three years after the cause of injury becomes known.

19 What are the consequences to an organization if an employee wins a civil action against them?

The employer would need to pay damages or compensation and these can run into some substantial amounts. Employers' liability insurance will cover the cost of the claims less any excess that the employer will pay. However, bear in mind that if the company has breached any Acts or regulations under statutory law then resultant fines are not insurable. There is also the poor publicity, which could lead to the loss of reputation and earnings.

The company then has to absorb the uninsured costs, which account for the main costs of an accident, into the company overheads. These costs are in addition to what is recoverable through insurance, and could include:

- lost time and talent of the injured employee;
- lost time and talent of other employees (poor morale);
- lost production (down time);
- cost of investigation and highlighting of other deficiencies;
- cost of medical centre and first-aid facilities;
- damage to property, plant and machinery;
- court expenditure and possible fines;
- cost of industrial unrest;
- cost of advertising and replacing lost labour;
- payments to injured employees;
- poor publicity and public relations;
- increased insurance premiums.

All internal risks should be within the organization's control and represent corporate risks to the organization. According to the HSE the average number of reportable incidents in a factory employing 500 people is 15 per year, and the indirect costs hugely outnumber the insured costs. There is a major economic benefit to organizations in managing health and safety as an integral part of the organization by using good risk management practices.

20 Who enforces health and safety legislation in the UK?

The Health and Safety Executive enforces the legislation in the following types of environments:

- industrial premises;
- factories;
- construction sites;
- mines and quarries;
- broadcasting and filming;
- airports;
- universities and colleges;
- shipping;
- railways;
- oil rigs;
- local authority premises;
- hospitals and nursing homes;
- agricultural activities.

The local authorities use inspectors from their environmental health departments to enforce in the following areas:

- retailers;
- exhibitions;

- caravan and camping sites;
- zoos and animal sanctuaries;
- childcare businesses;
- residential care;
- offices;
- catering services;
- baths and saunas;
- churches and religious buildings.

The powers that the HSE and local authorities have are the same, but the way that they use those powers can differ.

21 What powers do the inspectors have?

The inspectors can take action when they encounter a breach of health and safety legislation, or where they think that there may be an imminent risk of serious injury. They could, for example, issue an improvement notice if they are of the opinion that the company is contravening one or more statutory provisions, or has contravened and looks like it may do so again.

The inspector must be able to identify one or more legal requirements under an Act or regulation that have been contravened, e.g. not using machine guards, or not following a safe system of work as identified in a risk assessment. The improvement notice must:

- state the statutory provisions that have been contravened,
- specify the steps to remedy the situation, and
- specify a time within which the remedies should take place.

The time allowed is at least 21 days because there is an appeal procedure against the service of an improvement notice, and the appeal should be brought within the 21 days. The notice will be served on the employer's registered office and is usually served on the company secretary.

However, if the inspector believes that health and safety issues are so badly managed that there is an imminent risk of serious injury then a prohibition notice can be served. The notice must:

- state the inspector's opinion that there is a risk of serious injury,
- specify what creates the risk,
- state which statutory provisions are contravened, and
- state that the activities described in the notice cannot be carried out with immediate effect (this can be deferred to a specified time), until the provisions listed in the notice have been remedied.

22 What if a company fails to comply with the notices?

This is a criminal offence under Section 2 of the Health and Safety at Work etc. Act 1974, and legal proceedings would be issued against the employer on whom the notice was served. Failure to comply with an improvement notice carries a fine of up to £20,000 in a magistrate's court or an unlimited fine in Crown Courts, plus possible imprisonment.

Failure to comply with a prohibition notice could also result in a fine of up to £20,000 or an unlimited fine in the Crown Court.

If an employer continues to use defective equipment where a notice has been served (for example on defective machinery) then this would be a very serious offence indeed, and would likely incur a heavy fine and imprisonment.

23 So, what is the appeal process against these notices?

A company can appeal on any of the following grounds:

- the inspector wrongly interpreted the law;
- the inspector exceeded their powers;
- the proposed solution is not practicable;
- the breach of law is very insignificant and the risk is low.

An appeal must be lodged with an employment tribunal within 21 days of the notice being served. An improvement notice is suspended pending the appeal, but a prohibition notice remains in force pending the appeal.

24 Can an improvement notice be extended?

Yes. The inspector who served the notice can extend the time limits if the works cannot be completed in time and a request is submitted to the enforcing authority.

25 Are there any additional powers that an inspector has?

Yes, under the Health and Safety at Work etc. Act 1974 the inspectors have wide-ranging powers, and in addition to serving notices they can:

- enter and search premises,
- seize articles, substances or equipment,
- take measurements, photographs and recordings including interviews with staff and witnesses,
- detain items for testing,
- take samples for analysis,
- instruct that premises and anything in them remain undisturbed for as long as the investigation warrants it, and
- require for inspection documents such as risk assessments, training records and safety policies.

The inspectors may be accompanied by a police officer, and it is an offence to obstruct an inspector whilst carrying out their duties. An interview can take place under Section 20 of the Health and Safety at Work etc. Act 1974, and will take the form of questions being asked and answers being written down. These answers are non-voluntary statements and the person must answer the questions to the best of their ability. Although these statements can be used only against the company and not the individual during court proceedings, it is a criminal offence to knowingly give false answers to questions posed during the interview. The witness can read over the document before it is signed and dated, but they are not entitled to a copy of this document.

An interview can also take place under caution if the interviewee gives an answer that incriminates him or her as a person who may be subject to prosecution. The witness would be cautioned that he or she has given an answer that has cast suspicion upon him or herself. They are then formally cautioned before any further statements are taken.

If a manager has condoned unsafe working practices then he or she would be judged to be subject to prosecution and formally cautioned in this particular manner. The reality of being questioned face-to-face in this manner can be very stressful indeed, and anyone interviewed might be very nervous, particularly if they have never been involved in an incident before.

Case study

A food manufacturer was hit with a £100,000 fine after a worker was crushed to death in a health and safety accident. The company admitted breaching the Health and Safety at Work etc. Act 1974 and was issued the fine by the criminal court – companies considering training on Corporate Manslaughter should take note.

The incident took place in early 2006. An employee was working in the firm's packing department when a machine used to transfer cans to a conveyor belt became jammed. The employee crawled into the machine in an attempt to fix it, but its pneumatic pick-up units pinned him to a stack of trays, with the continued pressure on his chest leading him to die of asphyxiation.

The court found that there were 'serious and deliberate deficiencies' in the machine's safeguarding. The photoelectric light curtains had been wired out and the interlock on the hinged access gate to the machine enclosure had also been bypassed, allowing the machine to run with the guard door open.

This kind of failure highlights serious deficiencies in an organization's health and safety management system and a board's attitude towards the safety of their workforce.

The company should have had a detailed knowledge of machinery safety legislation and should have had a detailed maintenance procedure in place. They were also in breach of Regulation 11 of the Provision and Use of Work Equipment Regulations 1998, providing access to 'dangerous parts of machinery'.

The company should have implemented condition-based maintenance: this involves monitoring the condition of safety-critical parts, and carrying out maintenance before items can cause hazards. Compliance with the guarding standard BS EN 953, *Safety of machinery – Guards – General requirements for the design and construction of fixed and movable guards* would have avoided this accident, or with BS EN 1088, *Safety of Machinery – Interlocking devices associated with guards – Principles for design and selection*.

. . . .

4   The Supply of Machinery (Safety) Regulations 2008

1 Can you give me some background to the Machinery Directive?

All the EU member states are committed to the four freedoms defined in the 1956 Treaty of Rome: the freedom of movement of goods, services, finance and people. To achieve this, legislation relating to these freedoms clearly needed to be the same for all member states. Therefore, numerous European Directives, issued from Brussels, have been implemented into law across the EU by means of regulations. The UK implemented the original Machinery Directive 89/392/EEC into its legislation in the form of The Supply of Machinery (Safety) Regulations 1992, and it has been amended several times since. In December 2009 a new version of the Machinery Directive, 2006/42/EC, was implemented into UK law as The Supply of Machinery (Safety) Regulations 2008.

The regulations can look quite complex at first glance, but are in fact more straightforward than meets the eye. Essentially performing a dual function, the Machinery Directive not only promotes the free movement of machinery within the single market, but also guarantees a high level of protection to EU workers and citizens. It lists the potential hazards from machinery and requires that these be protected against. It lays down the essential health and safety requirements (EHSRs) which equipment covered by the regulations must meet, and calls upon EU member states to grant freedom of movement to equipment.

2 But what do the regulations require me to do?

Most importantly, they require all UK manufacturers and suppliers of new machinery to make sure that the machinery which they supply is safe. They also require manufacturers to make sure that, in addition to meeting the EHSRs:

- a technical file for the machinery has been drawn up. In certain cases, the machinery can be type-examined by a notified body to ensure compliance with the regulations. Some machinery, due to its design and intended use, is considered under the Machinery Directive 2006/42/EC to pose a continuing and significant risk to safety. Machinery of this type is listed in Annex IV of the Directive and includes products such as chainsaws, planers and presses amongst others. This kind of machinery is classed as high risk and the notified bodies are appointed by the member states. The principal role of a notified body is to offer services for conformity assessment on the conditions set out in the 'New Approach' Directives in support of CE marking. This support can involve conducting product examinations, documentation assessments or registering and storing technical files. The full list of notified bodies is published in the *Official Journal of the European Union* (*OJEU*);
- there is a 'declaration of conformity' (or in some cases a 'declaration of incorporation') for the machinery, which should be issued with the machinery;
- there is CE marking affixed to the machinery (unless it comes with a declaration of incorporation).

3 Does this Directive apply to all EU countries?

Yes, as explained in Chapter 3, a Directive must be implemented as national law in all countries in the European Economic Area (EEA), and this includes the Machinery Directive. This means that the same legal requirements now apply to all new machinery wherever it is supplied within the EEA.

4 So if I am importing a machine from a manufacturer based in another country in the EEA, what do I have to do?

You need to make sure that the machinery is safe before you supply it on to others, or even if you are the end user. Whether you rely on the competency of your staff to ensure that the machinery is safe or engage the services of a consultant, the responsibility remains yours.

5 What if I am directly importing machinery manufactured outside the EEA?

Machinery imported into the UK from outside the EEA must still meet the Supply of Machinery (Safety) Regulations 2008, and because you are importing it directly, you take on the legal responsibilities of the manufacturer. This means you need to make sure either that the manufacturer has met the relevant requirements or that you meet them yourself. You also need to make sure that the manufacturer has appointed an authorized representative within the EEA and that the representative's contact details are available should the authorities ever request to see the technical file. An authorized representative here means a person established within the EEA appointed by the manufacturer (whether or not established in the EEA) to act on the manufacturer's behalf in fulfilling obligations under the provisions of the Directive being applied. This representative must legally fulfil the role of retaining the conformity documentation and issuing the declaration of conformity (DoC) for products that carry the CE marking.

Care must be taken when importing machinery, whether from within or outside the EU, as different countries and manufacturers follow different interpretations of the Directive. This could potentially mean that you can import a machine to the UK that does not meet the same safety standards that would be expected in the UK.

Case study

A Japanese manufacturer of electronic 'pick and place' machines wanted to expand its business into Europe. The existing product was fine for the Japanese market, but the company's directors discovered that the CE mark was necessary before the machines could be used within the European Union; otherwise, they would be in breach of criminal law in the UK and subject to large fines and prohibition notices from the enforcement authorities.

The machines needed modifications to comply with EU regulations – specifically, the Low Voltage Directive, the Machinery Directive and the Electromagnetic Compatibility Directive. The modifications were carried out using supporting European and International Standards, as this was the simplest and easiest way of complying.

A review of the machinery designs was required, with an assessment to ensure that the equipment met the essential health and safety requirements set down in the regulations. The electrical system needed substantial modification, as this had to comply with BS EN 60204-1, *Safety of machinery – Electrical equipment of machines – General requirements* (the wire colours were all different and confusing), whilst the safety-related control circuitry had to comply with BS EN 954-1, *Safety of machinery – Safety related parts of control systems – Part 1: General principles for design*,[1] with a category 3 system.

---

[1] BS EN 954-1 is set to be superseded by BS EN ISO 13849-1, *Safety of machinery – Safety-related parts of control systems – General principles for design*. The two standards currently run alongside each other and both can be used to support compliance with the Machinery Directive.

The guards on the machines also had to be looked at, as there was access to moving parts, in breach of Regulation 11 of The Provision and Use of Work Equipment Regulations 1998. Upgrades to the guards were implemented using both BS EN 953, *Safety of machinery – Guards – General requirements for the design and construction of fixed and movable guards*, and BS EN 1088, *Safety of machinery – Interlocking devices associated with guards – Principles for design and selection*, for fitting door interlocks.

One other key decision by the Japanese company was to make an agreement with a company based in the EEA to act on their behalf as the authorized representative, and whose name and address would be used on the declaration of conformity.

The machines now satisfactorily comply with the Directives.

- -

6 What if I export machinery to countries outside the EEA?

You will need to find out the national requirements of the country to which you are exporting the machinery. While EU Directives might not apply, it is advisable to adhere to EU standards as a minimum, as well as any requirements specific to the country importing the machinery.

Case study

- -

A UK manufacturer of machinery (electric saws with a safety guard) was looking to expand into the US market. The company was advised by a consultant that in order to sell into the US, all the company had to do was meet the relevant US standards as no CE marking was required.

This is a commonly held view; however, the company sought the advice of another consultant who advised differently: the company could *not* take certain safety precautions in the UK but lesser precautions in the US – even though the product met US standards! To do so would compromise the company's legal defence if it ever needed one, and could potentially lead to damages. It was good risk management that led the company to investigate more fully the entry requirements for the US market. This investigation then led to a different outcome based on the consultant's advice, as even the cost of defending a case was too much to contemplate.

No UK business should choose to meet lower standards for the US, or any other non-EEA market, just because no CE marking is required. This notion of manufacturing to two different standards can attract unwanted attention from the authorities.

The company intentionally chose (with their clients in agreement) the use of European safety standards as the minimum requirement for all of their new products. Consequently, all new products will automatically have a Machinery Directive technical file, a declaration of conformity, and CE marking.

However, the ever-increasing use of international standards is an advantage, and these were implemented along with internationally accepted EN standards.

Moreover, it has been noted in recent years that more American companies are choosing to use EN standards as state of the art in the US marketplace. Some machine builders feel that working to UK manufacturing standards gives them a competitive advantage.

. . . .

7 Is there a law that applies to the sale of second-hand machinery?

The Supply of Machinery (Safety) Regulations 2008 only apply to the first supply of machinery into the EEA, when the machinery is placed on the market for the first time. Therefore, if you are supplying second-hand machinery which was first in use before 1993 (which was the date of the original Machinery Directive) without substantially refurbishing it, the machinery does not need to comply with these regulations. Unless this pre-1993 machinery was being imported into the EEA for the first time (irrespective of its age) some years after the original manufacturing date, it will need to comply with the Machinery Directive 2006/42/EC and any other applicable Directive at the time of supply and be CE marked. Also, if you are re-supplying used CE-marked machinery, these regulations do not apply. However, all machinery should be maintained in a safe state, and Section 6 of the Health and Safety at Work etc. Act 1974 will apply to the re-sale (in UK) of all second-hand workplace machinery, however old it is.

8 What if the old machinery I am supplying has been substantially refurbished?

Be careful here! If machinery has been refurbished to such an extent that almost all the replaceable parts are new, it would be considered to be new machinery and so you will need to comply with the Supply of Machinery (Safety) Regulations 2008 – but this can be a grey area. For example, where computer numerical controls (CNC) are retrofitted to an older manual lathe, these regulations apply. But if old machinery has simply had some parts replaced and been repainted, this would not make it 'new' and the regulations will not apply when it is re-sold. However, Section 6 of the Health and Safety at Work etc. Act 1974 *will* apply, as that is the ultimate law of the land as far as health and safety goes.

9 What are the relevant requirements of Section 6 of the Health and Safety at Work etc. Act 1974?

Section 6 of this Act places a duty on:

> *any person who designs, manufactures, imports or supplies*
> *any article for use at work … to ensure, so far as is reasonably*

practicable, that the article is so designed and constructed that it will be safe and without risks to health.

Adequate information about the use for which the article is designed is also required. These requirements must be met by suppliers of all types of workplace machinery, whether the machinery is new or second-hand. But the drawing up of a technical file, type-examination, the issuing of a declaration of conformity and affixing CE marking are not required under this Act. This is an explicit requirement of the Machinery Directive, and the two should not be confused.

10 Are there other laws that might be relevant to the supply of machinery?

Two sets of regulations that often apply are the Electrical Equipment (Safety) Regulations 1994 (Low Voltage Directive 73/23/EC), which apply to most electrically powered machinery used in workplaces, and the Electromagnetic Compatibility Regulations 2006 (EMC Directive 2004/108/EC), which cover equipment likely to cause electromagnetic disturbance, or whose performance is likely to be affected by electromagnetic disturbance.

11 So, how does the manufacturer make sure that machinery can be used safely?

There are several procedures which they must follow, but in particular they should:

- identify the health and safety hazards, both mechanical and non-mechanical (trapping, crushing, electrical shock, dust or fumes, noise, vibration, etc.), that are likely to be present when the machinery is used;

- assess the likely risks by doing a risk assessment; this can be done using BS EN ISO 14121-1, *Safety of Machinery – Risk assessment – Principles* which sets out principles for risk assessment;
- eliminate the risks, or if that is not possible
  - provide safeguards (e.g. guarding dangerous parts of the machinery, providing noise enclosures) or, if that is not possible
  - provide information about any residual risks and place signs on the machinery to warn of risks that cannot be reduced in other ways (e.g. 'noisy machine' signs).

Manufacturers may wish to refer to standards or other specifications when designing machinery, as they have been written to help manufacturers comply with legislation.

12 Does new machinery have to be made to conform to any particular standards?

No. Machinery must satisfy the essential health and safety requirements of the law, i.e. the Supply of Machinery (Safety) Regulations 2008 in the UK. But there are an increasing number of harmonized European standards that will help manufacturers to do this. Manufacturers have the option of addressing either the relevant European standards (listed in the *Official Journal of the European Union*) applicable to the product or ensuring that their product meets the essential health and safety requirements (EHSRs) listed in the Directive.

A harmonized European Standard has an EN before the number, e.g. EN 474-1, and is published in the UK as a British Standard, e.g. BS EN 474-1:2006. The use of these standards is voluntary, and manufacturers can design and manufacture their machinery in accordance with other national or international standards if they wish, so long as the essential health and safety requirements of the law are satisfied. In other words, those standards are 'best advice' documents, and don't form any part of our legal system. However, they have been written to enable us to meet the regulations, and compliance enables the manufacturer to self-certify their machinery.

13 Is the CE marking a guarantee of safety?

No, certainly not – but too many people take it for granted that it is! CE marking is not a quality mark, and affixing it on machinery is only one of several requirements that the manufacturer has to meet. By affixing CE marking to machinery the manufacturer is claiming that all relevant legal requirements have been met, but as the purchaser you must still make sure as far as possible that the machinery is safe, by inspecting it under the Provision and Use of Work Equipment Regulations 1998 when you receive it, and before you put it into use for the first time.

14 What if the machinery is manufactured by someone else either in the UK or elsewhere in the EEA and I (as a supplier) consider that the safeguards or other protective devices are inadequate?

There could be several reasons why this might happen. For example, the harmonized European Standard for that machinery may not yet have been agreed, and different interpretations of the level of protection that is required may exist in different countries. Alternatively, it may be that the machinery does not meet agreed levels of protection and the law is clearly not being met. If you are not satisfied with the levels of protection of the machinery you are supplying, discuss the matter with the manufacturer or your UK Trade Association.

Establishing clear design parameters with the manufacturer in the first place will help avoid such problems arising.

15 What is a technical file, and what should be included in it?

Before issuing a European Community (EC) declaration of conformity (certificate) it is essential that the manufacturer construct a technical file. The technical file does not have to be located in the territory of an EEA state, nor does it have to be permanently available in material form. However, it must be capable of being assembled and made available within a period of time commensurate with its complexity by the person designated in the EC declaration of conformity. The person designated in the declaration of conformity may be the authorized representative appointed by a manufacturer from outside of the EEA.

If a competent national authority asks that full documentation be presented, it will suffice that this documentation is compiled and made available in a reasonable time frame.

The technical file must include:

- a general description of the machinery;
- an overall drawing of the machinery, with drawings of the control circuits (schematics);
- full detailed drawings, any design calculations, functional test data, etc. required for checking conformity of the machinery with the EHSRs;
- a list of the EHSRs;
- the documentation on risk assessment demonstrating the procedure followed;
- a list of the essential health and safety requirements which apply to the machinery,

- a description of the protective measures implemented to eliminate identified hazards or to reduce risks and, when appropriate, the indication of the residual risks associated with the machinery;
- a copy of the instructions for the machinery;
- a declaration of conformity including the appropriate safety standards;
- where appropriate, the declaration of incorporation for partly completed machinery and the relevant assembly instructions;
- certificates obtained from notified or competent bodies (where needed);
- technical reports that declare conformity with a harmonized standard;
- operating and maintenance manuals;
- for series manufacturers, the internal measures that will be implemented to ensure that the machinery remains in conformity with this Directive.

16 When neither the manufacturer nor their authorized local representative fulfils the obligations of the Machinery Directive, who is responsible for CE marking the equipment?

These obligations shall fall to any persons placing machinery or safety components on the EU market. The same obligations shall apply to any person assembling machinery or parts thereof, or safety components of various origins, or constructing machinery or safety components for their own use. If they build for their own use then they are still considered to be supplying into the EU for the first time.

17 What language is acceptable for the instructions for the machinery?

The instructions must be written in one of the EU languages and the language of the country where the equipment is being supplied. So, all machinery placed into service must be accompanied by a translation of the instructions into the language or languages of the country in which the machinery is to be used. The translation must be done by the manufacturer, by the authorized representative in the EU, or by the person introducing the machinery into the area. A good move is always to supply an English copy and another in the language of the end user.

18 Where can the technical file be kept?

The Machinery Directive 2006/42/EC permits the manufacturer to keep the documents. Technical files (TFs) must be kept for at least 10 years after the last date of manufacture of the product. The TF can be drawn up in one of the official languages of the EU, with the exception of the instructions for the machinery, as these need to be in the language of the user. Technical documentation can be kept electronically; however, it must be possible to assemble it and make it available within a reasonable period of time. Bear in mind that if you have a computer crash then you may lose all your data for the TF! A good risk management procedure would be to have an additional copy elsewhere in a safe place, stored on a separate memory disk.

19 When will machinery be issued with a declaration of conformity?

When it is completed and ready for installation and use. The machine will meet the definition of a machine as set out in Part 2 Regulation 4 of The Supply of Machinery (Safety) Regulations 2008, and operate with an independent power source.

20 What should a declaration of conformity have on it?

A declaration of conformity must include:

- the name and full address of the manufacturer;
- where appropriate, the name and address of the manufaturer's authorized representative;
- the name and address of the person authorized to complete the technical file, who must be established within any EEA state;
- a description and identification of the machinery, including generic denomination, function, model, type, serial number and commercial name;
- a sentence expressly declaring that the machinery fulfils all the relevant provisions of the Directive and, where appropriate, a similar sentence declaring conformity with other Directives and/ or relevant provisions with which the machinery complies;
- an indication of all relevant European laws (Directives) with which the machinery complies;
- the details of any notified body that has been involved in certifying compliance, if any;
- details of which standards have been used in the manufacture (if any);
- the place and date of the declaration;
- the signature of an authorized person.

For machinery supplied in the UK, the declaration of conformity must be in English. For machinery exported to other countries in the EEA, instructions must be in the recognized language of the country where it is to be used.

21 When is a declaration of incorporation appropriate rather than a declaration of conformity?

If the machinery is intended for incorporation into other machinery or for assembly with other machinery, and if certain other conditions are met, the manufacturer may issue a declaration of incorporation instead of a declaration of conformity. The declaration should contain similar information to that contained in the declaration of conformity; but, importantly, it must state that the machinery should not be used until the machinery into which it has been incorporated, or the assembly to which it has been added, has been declared to conform fully with the legal requirements.

In practice, this means that the machinery should not be used until the final product has been manufactured, all relevant essential health and safety requirements met, and a declaration of conformity issued by the final installer or assembler.

The machinery *should not be CE marked* if it has a declaration of incorporation; CE marking should only take place at the end of incorporation or assembly.

22 I understand that the Directive has recently been revised: are there any changes we need to be aware of?

The revised Machinery Directive, 2006/42/EC, does not introduce any radical changes compared with the previous Directive, 98/37/EC, but aims to consolidate its achievements in terms of free circulation and safety of machinery while improving its application.

The Machinery Directive 2006/42/EC was published on 9 June 2006 and came into force on 29 June 2006. EU member states had until 29 June 2008 to adopt and publish the national laws and regulations transposing the provisions of the new Directive into national law.

The provisions of the new Directive became applicable on 29 December 2009.

The scope of the Machinery Directive is extended, since construction-site hoists and cartridge-operated fixing and other impact machinery will no longer be excluded.

Essential health and safety requirements

The essential health and safety requirements have not been subject to major changes, although several of them have been redrafted. Among the significant changes:

- the requirement relating to risk assessment has been made more explicit, as there tended to be an 'implicit requirement' before;
- there are new requirements for risks associated with machinery serving fixed landings, to take account of the extension of the scope of the Directive to construction-site hoists and slow-moving lifts;
- certain requirements currently applicable to mobile machinery or machinery for lifting are made applicable to all machinery presenting the risk concerned;
- requirements concerning noise and vibration emissions are made more precise;
- the integration of safety devices must now take into account any reasonably foreseeable misuse of such devices;
- the different life phases have been detailed, and now include transport, assembly, dismantling, disabling and scrapping as well as the normal use phase.

Conformity assessment procedures

As under the previous Machinery Directive 98/37/EC, the conformity of most machinery will continue to be certified by the manufacturers themselves.

The list of categories of machinery subject to particular conformity assessment procedures is set out in Annex IV of the Machinery Directive; however, manufacturers of Annex IV machinery will have a wider choice of procedure.

For Annex IV machinery designed according to harmonized standards covering all the relevant essential requirements, the manufacturers will be able to certify the conformity of the machinery themselves.

For other Annex IV machinery, the manufacturers will be able to choose between EC type-examination by a notified body, or approval by a notified body of the manufacturers' full quality assurance system.

The new Machinery Directive 2006/42/EC includes an obligation for the EU member states to monitor the performance of notified bodies and to withdraw or suspend the notification if a body fails to carry out its duties properly.

23 Is it mandatory to use a notified body for testing?

It used to be under the old Directive; however, Annex IV in the new Machinery Directive 2006/42/EC provides a list of machinery categories that must comply with certain conformity assessment procedures. Fortunately, manufacturers of Annex IV machinery will now have three procedures from which to choose, as stated in the answer to Question 22. It is important to note that, under the new Directive, EU member states constantly review notified bodies. If a notified body does not pass muster, then the member state can withdraw or suspend its notification.

The following machinery is covered by Annex IV:

- circular saws, sawing machines;
- hand-fed surface planing machines for woodworking;

- band saws;
- combined wood working machines;
- hand-fed vertical spindle moulding machines;
- portable chain saws;
- presses including press breaks for cold working of metals;
- injection or compression machines for plastics or rubber moulding;
- machinery for underground work (e.g. machinery on rails, hydraulic-powered roof supports, or internal combustion engines);
- manually loaded trucks for collection of household refuse incorporating compression mechanisms;
- guards and detachable transmission shafts with universal joints;
- vehicle-servicing lifts;
- devices for lifting persons who are at risk of falling more than three metres;
- machines for the manufacture of pyrotechnics.

24 Does CE + CE = CE?

This is a question that is often asked by clients, but what do they mean by this?

Very simply, they are asking whether if the end user has bought, for example, two separate machines (CE marked independently) but interlinked together in any way (e.g. electrically or mechanically, as in a production line), is there any need to CE mark the whole system?

The answer is that, unfortunately, it is not as simple as assuming that the two CE-marked machines would meet the requirements of the Machinery Directive. Many final production line assemblies contain complex electrical and/or electronic items that have been purchased from other suppliers, for example a robot to operate as part of a complete production line. Finished systems and installations are usually constructed from bought-in finished products and systems, such as computers, instrumentation and control equipment and machinery.

The 'CE + CE = CE' approach cannot in fact give any confidence in achieving due diligence, and leads to uncontrolled business risks (although in some circumstances it is capable of achieving a presumption of conformity). Just remember that liability for non-compliance cannot easily be passed on to the supplier of a non-compliant item. So, where a final machine is found to be non-compliant by reason of the non-compliance of an incorporated item, enforcement agencies (the Health and Safety Executive in this case) are likely to take action against both the final manufacturer and the supplier of the item.

When suppliers sign their declarations of conformity and affix the CE mark to their products, some may not quite exercise the due diligence that their customers require. Other suppliers may have tried conscientiously to meet their legal obligations, but made serious errors. Bear in mind that in either case, the responsibility lies with the end user who assembles the entire process line. The user should re-mark the whole line, even if some of the equipment being incorporated has already been CE marked by the supplier.

5 The Provision and Use of Work Equipment Regulations 1998

1 What is the background to the Provision and Use of Work Equipment Regulations 1998?

The Use of Work Equipment Directive 89/655/EEC concerns the minimum health and safety requirements for the use of work equipment by workers at work.

It places obligations on businesses and employers to take into account potential dangers to operators and other persons using or affected by machines and equipment, and confers responsibility for ensuring that new, second-hand and existing equipment is safe, suitable for use and fit for the purpose intended, that it has been correctly installed and is properly used and maintained.

The Directive is implemented into UK law under The Health and Safety at Work etc. Act 1974 as The Provision and Use of Work Equipment Regulations 1998 (PUWER 98), and covers equipment ranging from power presses and fork-lift trucks to photocopiers and hand tools. It is sometimes termed the 'user law', as it applies to existing work equipment.

PUWER 98 imposes strict liability on an employer to keep work equipment in good repair, and requires that risks to people's health and safety from equipment that they use at work are prevented or controlled. In addition to the requirements of PUWER 98, lifting equipment is also subject to the requirements of The Lifting Operations and Lifting Equipment Regulations 1998.

2 What equipment is covered by the regulations then?

Generally, any equipment which is used by an employee at work is covered, for example hammers, knives, ladders, drilling machines, power presses, circular saws, photocopiers, lifting equipment (including lifts), dumper trucks and motor vehicles. Similarly, if you allow employees to provide their own equipment, e.g. an electrically powered calculator or microwave, it too will be covered by PUWER 98 and you will need to make sure it complies. That is the employer's responsibility.

Work equipment must meet all the requirements of the regulations from 5 December 1998. However, requirements relating to certain aspects of mobile work equipment that had been provided for use in the business before 5 December 1998 did not apply until 5 December 2002. HSE information sheet MISC156 should be read if you use hired mobile work equipment.

Examples of uses of equipment which are covered by the regulations include starting or stopping the equipment, repairing, modifying, maintaining, servicing, cleaning and transporting it.

3 Who does PUWER 98 apply to?

If you are an employer or self-employed person and you provide equipment for use at work, or if you have control of the use of equipment, then the regulations will apply to you. They do not apply to equipment used by the public, for example compressed air equipment used in a garage forecourt. However, such circumstances are covered by the Health and Safety at Work etc. Act 1974.

While your employees do not have duties under PUWER 98, they do have general duties under the Health and Safety at Work etc. Act 1974 (Sections 7 and 8) and The Management of Health and Safety at Work Regulations 1999: for example, to take reasonable care of themselves and others who may be affected by their actions, and to co-operate with others.

The regulations cover places where the Health and Safety at Work etc. Act 1974 applies, and these include factories, offshore installations, offices, shops, hospitals, hotels and places of entertainment. PUWER 98 also applies in common parts of shared buildings and temporary places of work, such as construction sites. While the regulations cover equipment used by people working from home, they do not apply to domestic work in a private household.

4 What does PUWER 98 require me to do?

You must ensure that the work equipment you provide meets the requirements of PUWER 98. In doing so, you should ensure that it is:

- suitable for use, and for the purpose and conditions in which it is used;
- maintained in a safe condition for use so that people's health and safety is not at risk;
- inspected in certain circumstances to ensure that it is, and continues to be, safe for use.

Inspections on work equipment should always be carried out by a competent person (this could be an employee as long as they have the necessary competence to perform the task) and a record kept until the next inspection.

You should also ensure that risks, created by the use of the equipment, are eliminated where possible or controlled by taking appropriate:

- 'hardware' measures, e.g. providing suitable guards, protection devices, markings and warning devices, system control devices (such as emergency stop buttons) and personal protective equipment, and
- 'software' measures, such as following safe systems of work and procedures (e.g. ensuring maintenance is only performed when equipment is shut down), and providing adequate information, instruction and training.

A combination of these measures may be necessary depending on the requirements of the work, your assessment of the risks involved, and the practicability of such measures. You need to ensure that people using work equipment have received adequate training, instruction and information for the particular equipment.

Mobile work equipment

In addition to these general requirements, which apply to all work equipment, Part III of PUWER 98 contains specific duties regarding mobile work equipment, for example forklift trucks and dumper trucks. You should ensure that where mobile work equipment is used for carrying people, it is suitable for this purpose. Measures should be taken to reduce the risks (e.g. from it rolling over) to the safety of the people being carried, the operator and anyone else.

Power presses

Part IV of the regulations also contains specific requirements regarding power presses. In particular, you should have a power press, and associated guard or protection device, thoroughly examined at specified intervals and inspected daily in use to ensure that it is safe. A competent person should perform this work, and records should be kept.

Case study

A large power generation company had decided to upgrade two very large (and very old) overhead cranes in different power stations as they approached the summer outages, when the cranes would be needed for plant maintenance.

The cranes were over fifty years old, and a survey from a crane consultant specialist found that some physical changes and strengthening were necessary. It was also noted by the machinery safety consultant that the machine electrics and safety circuitry needed complete refurbishment. There was a risk that if the cranes didn't get upgraded then repairs during the outages could not go ahead, potentially putting key items of plant at risk. If the plant failed to operate then naturally the company wouldn't be able to generate electricity from this particular power station.

There was no need to comply with the Machinery Directive on CE marking as the cranes were so old, but there was a need to comply with the Provision and Use of Work Equipment Regulations 1998, and with the Lifting Operations and Lifting Equipment Regulations 1998. A complete overhaul of the cranes was required, and a good starting point was the crane standard, BS 7121-1:2006, *Code of practice for safe use of cranes – General*, whilst the electrics were refurbished in accordance with BS EN 60204-32:2008, *Safety of machinery – Electrical equipment of machines – Requirements for hoisting machines*.

A radio controlled console unit was used to perform the emergency stop function and, in accordance with BS EN 13557, *Cranes – Controls and control stations*, it was specified to category 3 for system performance.

A risk assessment was also carried out for the whole cranes that showed the areas of non-compliance, and recommendations were made to bring the crane up to modern-day safety standards and thus meet the legal requirements.

The refurbishment saved the company around £50,000, and emphasizes the importance of having a good knowledge of what is required by both regulations and associated standards.

··

5 How does PUWER 98 compare and relate to other health and safety legislation?

The requirements of the regulations need to be considered alongside other health and safety law. For example, Section 2 of the Health and Safety at Work etc. Act 1974 requires all employers to ensure, so far as is reasonably practicable, the health, safety and welfare of all their employees. Similarly, the Management of Health and Safety at Work Regulations 1999 contain important duties relating to the carrying out of a risk assessment (Regulation 3) to identify measures that employers can take to eliminate, or reduce, the risks presented by the particular hazards in their workplaces.

Other, more specific legislation may equally apply, such as The Workplace (Health, Safety and Welfare) Regulations 1992, which cover, for example, workplace risks to pedestrians from vehicles, and The Construction (Design and Management) Regulations 2007, which contain specific requirements relating to certain types of work equipment such as scaffolding.

Generally, if you are meeting the requirements of more specific legislation such as those outlined above, then this should normally be sufficient to meet the more general requirements of PUWER 98.

6 How do employees ensure the safe use of work equipment or machinery?

Employees should always check that:

- they are familiar with the operation of the machine;
- they know how to stop the machine before they even start it;
- all guards are in position and all protective devices are in working order, e.g. light guards or interlocking guards;
- the area around the machine is tidy and free from obstruction, i.e. good housekeeping;
- they are wearing appropriate personal protective equipment if required.

7 What sort of training would an enforcement officer expect my company to undertake?

Enforcement officers will expect to see documented training plans and schedules which will achieve the employer's objectives in meeting health and safety legislation. Employers should bear in mind the goal of the Health and Safety Commission, that: 'Everyone at work should be competent to fulfil his or her roles in controlling risk.'

Case study

A worker received an electric shock whilst working on a faulty machine (this was a maintenance activity), and was awarded an out of court settlement of £40,000. He had simply relied on electro-mechanical interlock switches to isolate the machine (as opposed to locking off the main isolating switch). The company had failed to ensure that all equipment was isolated before employees began to carry out maintenance activities.

This was a breach of The Provision and Use of Work Equipment Regulations 1998: Regulation 19, Isolation from sources of energy. Following the incident, the company began to implement the risk assessment standard BS EN ISO 14121-1, *Safety of machinery – Risk assessment – Principles*, for every maintenance operation.

This gave the business the confidence that they were following the correct procedure by following the steps set out in a standard that has been specifically written in order to meet machinery and work equipment legislation. The standard also enabled the business to compile a 'Safe System of Work', which is a sequence of procedures followed in order to reduce or eliminate the risks from a hazard which, in itself, cannot be eliminated – in this particular case, the hazard was electricity.

If the company had followed this route in the first place, and devised their own forms with the logical steps, then the accident would have been prevented, enabling the operator to complete the task safely.

6 The use of harmonized standards

1 What is the background to harmonized standards?

Harmonized European standards have been in existence for many years and thousands are available, but in 1985 the EC Council of Ministers adopted a resolution setting out a new approach to the use of standards in EC law. Under this 'new approach', Directives made under Article 100a of the Treaty of Rome should set out the essential health and safety requirements (EHSRs) relating to safety, etc. EHSRs should be written in general terms, and must be satisfied before products may be sold in member states. Harmonization of the technical detail should be achieved by reference to relevant harmonized standards.

The standardisation bodies are usually the European Committee for Standardization (CEN) or the European Committee for Electrotechnical Standardization (CENELEC). The British Standards Institution (BSI) is the UK national standards body and member of these two European organizations, and HSE representatives frequently sit on BSI committees. Harmonized standards should follow general rules agreed between CEN/CENELEC and the EC. Having completed negotiation, such standards are published as Euronorms (EN) and, generally speaking, the authorities will assume that any machine manufactured to those standards will actually comply with the EHSRs.

2 What are the benefits of harmonized standards?

By complying with harmonized standards a machine builder (for example) could self-certify their equipment, saving cash and knowing that they are meeting at least the 'minimum standards' required by the regulations (this is *not* equivalent to 'best practice', as some people would try to claim!).

Work equipment legislation can be pretty complex and, while compliance with a standard does not automatically mean compliance with legislation, identifying the relevant standards and applying them correctly can help an organization meet its legal requirements. In addition, compliance with standards is a good selling point and can offer a competitive edge in the marketplace.

3 Why do standards always have different prefixes?

British, European and international standards cover the entire spectrum of products, services and processes, from administration to children's toys. The origin of standards can be identified as follows:

- all British standards use the product identifier 'BS';
- all European standards adopted as British standards are identified with 'BS EN';
- all international standards are identified with 'ISO';
- all international standards adopted as British standards are identified with 'BS ISO';
- all international standards adopted as European standards and then again as British standards are identified with 'BS EN ISO' (except those of IEC origin, which are published as part of the BS EN 60000 series).

4 What are some of the key machinery safety standards?

For safety-related electrical control circuits, BS EN 62061, *Safety of machinery – Functional safety of safety-related electrical, electronic and programmable electronic control systems* is now harmonized to the Machinery Directive and suitable for any manufacturer who wishes to use a safety programmable logic controller. Alternatively, they may wish to use BS EN ISO 13849-1, *Safety of machinery – Safety-related parts of control systems – General principles for design* for the safety-related control circuit. The big question is which of these two standards to use. The simple, logical step for anyone used to BS EN 954-1, *Safety of machinery – Safety related parts of control systems – Part 1: General principles for design* (the forerunner to BS EN ISO 13849-1) is to use BS EN ISO 13849-1; however, for electronic programmable controllers BS EN 62061 should be applied.

Although compliance with these standards is not a legal requirement, it could be extremely difficult for a machine builder to demonstrate compliance with the EHSRs of the Machinery Directive if the standards have not been followed.

BS EN 60204-1:2006, *Safety of machinery – Electrical equipment of machines – General requirements* is a revised version of the 1998 standard, and there are a number of differences to note. Most importantly, programmable electronic safety-related systems are now accepted by the standard, which effectively brings the standard up to date with the technological state of the art. Another notable change is Clause 5.4, which relates to devices for switching off and for the prevention of unexpected start-up: control isolation is now permitted in specific circumstances, such as for inspections or adjustments. Numerous lesser changes have also been made to the main body of the standard and the annexes, so anyone that claims to be working to the standard should make sure they have purchased and studied the latest version.

At the time of writing (December 2009), following a six-year transition period, BS EN 954-1, *Safety of machinery – Safety related parts of control systems – General principles for design* has been extended for an unspecified period of time, likely to be three years at most but possibly less. This standard will be superseded by BS EN ISO 13849-1. BS EN ISO 13849-1 is harmonized to the Machinery Directive 2006/42/EC.

Manufacturers should note that when BS EN 954-1 is eventually withdrawn, it will no longer provide a presumption of conformity. Until then, manufacturers have the choice which standard to use, although the more logical decision would be to use BS EN ISO 13849-1.

5 Can you give a brief overview on the classification of the machinery safety standards, as it seems complex?

These standards are classified into three sections: A, B and C.

The **A standards** simply apply to all machinery, and provide essential information for all machine builders. There are three A standards that relate to machine safety:

- BS EN 414, *Safety of Machinery – Rules for the drafting and presentation of safety standards* is the 'standard for standards', and evolved so that there could be conformity in the way safety standards are written.
- BS EN ISO 12100, *Safety of machinery – Basic concepts, general principles for design* comprises of two parts relating to terminology and methodology (Part 1) and technical principles (Part 2). This standard defines the basic concept of machine safety and specifies general principles and techniques to help machine designers achieve safety.

- BS EN ISO 14121-1, *Safety of machinery – Risk assessment – Principles* gives advice on how to assess the risk of injury or damage to health, so that appropriate safety measures can be selected.

The **B standards** are subdivided into two sections:

- Group B1 covers safety aspects for design, e.g. electrical equipment, safety distances, and safety-related controls. These standards always apply.
- Group B2 covers safety components and devices e.g. light barriers, pressure mats, laser scanners etc. These standards are applied when required.

The **C standards** apply to certain machines and inform manufacturers and users about the specific safety precautions they should take and the safety devices that they should use.

6 Can you tell us a bit more about those C standards?

C standards are very useful in that they tell you what the safety risks of the machinery are and indicate the minimum safety category or performance level – as in BS EN ISO 13849-1 – that should be used. However, as time goes on, these standards (such as BS EN 692, *Machine tools – Mechanical presses – Safety*) are being rewritten and produced as international ISO standards. These will contain references to BS EN ISO 13849-1 and BS EN 62061, rather than the old BS EN 954-1.

When designing a machine, it can save time to first check whether there is a C type standard available as this will detail all the requirements. More information on standards can be found on the BSI website, www.bsi-global.com.

7 Can you give some background information on BS EN ISO 13849-1:2008 that replaces BS EN 954-1, as that is a key machinery standard?

BS EN ISO 13849-1, *Safety of machinery – Safety-related parts of control systems – General principles for design* is harmonized to the Machinery Directive, and replaces BS EN 954-1 *Safety of machinery – Safety-related parts of control systems*, which was a standard that machine builders were familiar with and found fairly straightforward to use. However, BS EN 954-1 was a relatively simple standard, with an easy-to-follow risk graph that helped people establish a safety category for their machine. Safety categories are worked out on a qualitative basis, so the process is fairly quick. BS EN ISO 13849-1 follows a similar process to define a performance level as opposed to a category, but the user then has to perform a number of calculations involving diagnostic coverage, mean time to dangerous failure, architecture and common-cause failures to validate that the performance level has been achieved.

This quantitative approach is undoubtedly more appropriate for machinery, and it also enables the proposed safety-related control system to be validated. With BS EN 954-1 it was a case of designing the system and relying on the design being right, but BS EN ISO 13849-1 obliges you to validate the control system. You can then use BS EN ISO 13849-2, *Safety of machinery – Safety-related parts of control systems – General principles for design: Part 2 Validation*, which specifies the validation process, including both analysis and testing, for the safety functions and categories of safety-related parts of control systems. This is an essential process in the overall design of the system.

Case study

A company was setting up in Northern Ireland buying second-hand conveyor systems from a business in Germany. On receiving the equipment the NI business decided that the conveyors did not meet the legislation. This had been accepted in Germany but the Belfast-based business had to satisfy the UK enforcement authorities.

The company had to comply with the Health and Safety at Work etc. Act 1974, but also with The Supply of Machinery (Safety) Regulations 2008 as well as The Provision and Use of Work Equipment Regulations 1998. The new Health and Safety (Offences) Act 2008 had also been recently introduced in the UK, which increased the penalties that could be applied in the lower courts meaning higher potential penalties for UK businesses.

One or more methods of machine guarding were needed to protect the operator and other employees that would be working near the conveyor area from hazards such as those created by point of operation, ingoing nip points and rotating parts. Examples of guarding methods include barrier guards, two-hand tripping devices and electronic safety devices.

The company decided to implement the guarding standard EN 953, *Safety of machinery – Guards – General requirements for the design and construction of fixed and movable guards* as well as the interlocking standard BS EN 1088, *Safety of Machinery – Interlocking devices associated with guards – Principles for design and selection* to assist them in meeting their legal requirements. This allowed the company to follow a simple and logical process based on a hierarchy of control measures depending on the level of risk.

7 BS EN ISO 13849-1, *Safety of machinery – Safety-related parts of control systems – General principles for design*

1 Is BS EN ISO 13849-1 now an applicable machinery safety standard?

Yes, absolutely. BS EN ISO 13849-1, *Safety of machinery – Safety-related parts of control systems – General principles for design* is now a harmonized standard and it will replace the 'tried and tested' BS EN 954-1, *Safety of machinery – Safety related parts of control systems – Part 1: General principles for design* (see also Chapter 6, Questions 4 and 6). However, another standard called BS EN 62061, *Safety of machinery – Functional safety of safety-related electrical, electronic and programmable electronic control systems* also applies for the safe design and functionality of machinery using electrical, electronic, and programmable electronic control equipment. So, if someone is designing and including a programmable logic controller into the system then they would normally follow the latter standard, whereas BS EN ISO 13849-1 is used regardless of the type of energy source (e.g. electrical, pneumatic or hydraulic).

In addition, the publication of BS EN ISO 13849-2, *Safety of machinery – Safety-related parts of control systems – Validation*, gives machine builders a standard against which they can work when validating safety-related control systems, which is an essential process in the overall design of the system. The scope of BS EN ISO 13849-2 is relatively broad, encompassing the validation of safety-related parts of control systems that use mechanical, pneumatic, hydraulic and electrical (and electronic) technologies.

For complex systems, validation should be carried out by persons who are independent of the design of the safety-related parts.

A flow diagram in ISO 13849-2 shows the validation process, with the preparation of the validation plan coming first.

2 Why is BS EN ISO 13849-1 replacing BS EN 954-1?

BS EN 954-1 had reached its technological limits, and there were no reliability values for individual components or testing measures taken into account during the categorization process. However, because it was so easy and straightforward to use, and was widely accepted in the marketplace and with machine builders in particular, there was some opposition to the new standard. This new standard adds a quantitative calculation to the qualitative requirements of the previous standard, but will take some time to get used to. Once people get used to it, we will wonder what all the fuss was about!

3 Are there any similarities between the two standards?

Yes, of course there are. BS EN ISO 13849-1 incorporates the assessment criteria familiar from BS EN 954-1 when selecting categories (categories are still used within the scope of the standard, but only as part of the process of determining a performance level), but then builds upon that by looking at the reliability of the components, the quality of testing, etc. This means that the *number* of faults is no longer being counted, but rather the probability of their occurring, based on the device's characteristics. A risk graph is still used for estimating the level of performance required.

4 What approach can we take to simplify the new standard?

BS EN ISO 13849-1 essentially sets out a four-stage approach, as follows:

1 Perform a risk assessment using BS EN ISO 14121-1:2007, *Safety of machinery – Risk assessment – Principles*. This is essential, and is now an explicit requirement of the new Machinery Directive 2006/42/EC.
2 Then allocate the safety measure by arriving at a performance level using the risk graph from BS EN ISO 13849-1 (this is indeed quite similar to the old graph in BS EN 954-1).
3 Devise a system architecture that is suitable for the performance level.
4 Validate the design to ensure that it meets the initial risk assessment.

5 Where are the main differences between BS EN ISO 13849-1 and BS EN 62061?

Both of these standards were created around the same time, and the main differences between the two are that BS EN ISO 13849-1 is for machine construction and looks at safety-related parts of control circuitry, whereas BS EN 62061 mainly looks at the functional safety of safety-orientated electrical and electronic programmable systems. It is based on IEC 61508, *Functional safety of electrical/electronic/ programmable electronic safety-related systems*, so companies that already use this will actually have an easy transition here. BS EN 62061 uses safety integrity levels (SILs) to reduce risk (as opposed to the performance levels used in BS EN ISO 13849-1), where SIL1 is the lowest level of risk and SIL3 is the highest. Risks in other industries, such as the process sector, actually have a SIL4 for an even greater risk magnitude.

6 Why don't they just have the one standard for machines?

There could be efforts towards this in the future, but the fact is that both standards will probably be with us for quite a number of years now, and they both lead to a comparable safety effort anyway. It is like everything else, in that they just take a little bit of getting used to – but also bear in mind that they were both written by different technical committees.

7 So what standard should a machine builder use?

Well, for small to medium machines they could use BS EN ISO 13849-1, as that would be the logical and practical choice for smaller machines and covers all types of energy source such as electrical, hydraulic, etc. There are similarities between the new process of selecting performance levels and the old system of categories, but there is now an improvement in reliability and robustness. However, if there were a safety programmable logic controller (plc) involved then the logical choice would be to use BS EN 62061. Using either standard will enable a manufacturer to comply with the new Machinery Directive 2006/42/EC.

8 Is it just a case of selecting these performance levels in BS EN ISO 13849-1?

Not quite; as mentioned earlier in this chapter, there is a risk graph using the risk parameters of severity of injury, frequency of exposure, and possibility of avoiding the hazard – which is effectively what was done under the old standard. However, this simply allows you to arrive at a performance level of a, b, c, d or e, which is nearly identical to arriving at a category in BS EN 954-1. However, these levels then need to be validated. This is achieved through some mathematical calculations based on:

- diagnostic coverage, which is the fractional decrease in the probability of dangerous hardware failures;
- common cause failures, which is the probability of failure on a redundant system, that often equates to a single channel system; and
- mean time to dangerous failure.

It can take a bit of getting used to, but follow the four-step process described in the answer to Question 4.

9 So, this means that we can comply by using either of these two standards?

Yes, effectively you can for the time being. BS EN 954-1 remains valid as it has been extended for an unspecified period of time to provide a nice transitional period. However, it will be superseded by the two coexisting standards: BS EN ISO 13849-1 and BS EN 62061. Designers and installers can choose now between BS EN 954-1 or the new standards, BS EN ISO 13849-1 and BS EN 62061, and still comply with the Machinery Directive 2006/42/EC; but BS EN 954-1 will in the near future be rendered obsolete.

Case study
....

A manufacturer of auto component parts had applied BS EN 954-1, *Safety of machinery – Safety related parts of control systems – Part 1: General principles for design* for the safety-related parts of control circuitry for a number of years, but was now faced with making the change to either

BS EN ISO 13849-1, *Safety of machinery – Safety-related parts of control systems – General principles for design* or BS EN 62061, *Safety of machinery – Functional safety of safety-related electrical, electronic and programmable electronic control systems.* They had a choice to make. If they did not change to one or the other of the new standards (or both, depending on the equipment), then they could potentially be in breach of the new Machinery Directive 2006/42/EC when it came into effect on 29 December 2009 (the EC only granted a three year extension in September 2009).

They decided to learn both standards (by getting employees trained on an external course) as they used programmable logic controllers more often than not, and it was possible that a client could specify one or the other to them for a project. The risk was also too great if they decided to specialize in only one of the standards, as they would face a further learning curve that could result in financial losses or even a loss of contract if there was unfamiliarity with one of the standards.

Offering both standards to clients also gave them an edge in the market over their competitors; however, the company decided that as a first choice they would look at implementing BS EN 62061.

. . . .

8   High-risk environments

1 What do you class as a high-risk work environment?

As well as construction sites, there are even higher risk industries such as chemical laboratories, nuclear power plants, offshore installations and air transport. We are referring to the greater potential for the severity of harm here.

The first principle in the high-risk industries when evaluating hazards is to consider the potentially dangerous processes used, as well as the risks to the wider environment. In relation to these industries the principle risks are explosion, fire, and the release of radioactive and toxic materials.

2 What are the biggest hazards?

That is difficult to define, but you will find explosive and fire hazards in almost any industry, whilst toxic materials in some particular industries, such as chemical plants, can have unpredictable or even unquantifiable consequences.

The Bhopal Disaster in India is one example. The incident took place in the early hours of the morning of 3 December 1984, when 27 tonnes of methyl isocyanate (a poisonous gas) was released from a pesticide plant in the town of Bhopal, immediately killing at least 3,800 people. According to the Bhopal Medical Appeal, around half a million people were exposed to the gas: approximately 20,000 people, to this date, are believed to have died as a result, while over 120,000 continue to suffer ill-health such as breathing difficulties, cancer, serious birth-defects, blindness, gynaecological complications and other related problems. There was no contingency plan for evacuation in the event of an emergency.

Poor sales had led the company to cut costs, scale back production and lay off around a third of the workforce. It has been reported that safety systems had also been cut and that maintenance had fallen into a state of disrepair, although the exact causes of the disaster are disputed.

3 What does 'toxic' mean?

'Toxicity' refers to a material's ability to harm living things. Some toxic materials, or toxins, may irritate the nose, eyes, and skin. Others may damage the body's internal organs. Other toxins may cause suffocation, sterility, cancer or other diseases. Some can be immediately fatal. Some materials don't appear toxic at all to adults, but can seriously damage an unborn child, and others may cause cell mutations, creating abnormalities in future generations. Two things determine a material's toxicity: the amount of the material necessary to cause harm, and the possible extent of the damage. However, thousands of toxic materials are safely used in industry every day, and there is no need to fear them provided they are assessed and used with the proper control measures.

4 What about the physical nature of the substance?

The scale of the hazard does depend on the physical nature of the substance, for example they could be in solid, liquid or gaseous form. A toxic gas escape could be much more serious than in a solid, powder or liquid form.

5 How do you go about assessing a high-risk environment?

The fundamental principles of health, safety and risk management are much the same for all industries, whether they are high risk or not. The higher risk industries are singled out for the size and scope of the risks they pose for the environment and the wider public and the need to put in place systems to minimize risks.

6 What are the risks from radioactivity in the workplace?

Risks relating to radioactivity and related illnesses differ from explosion and fire, in that radioactivity is commonly associated exclusively with the nuclear industry. However, the nuclear industry is not the only source of radiation, as radon (a natural radioactive gas) seeps into buildings from minute amounts of uranium that are present in all rocks, soils, brick and concrete. Miners exposed to high radon levels have been found to run an increased risk of lung cancer. Radon in the home also presents a risk, but generally at a lower level.

Radon is present in all parts of the UK, but in the most populous areas the levels are quite low. Some of the highest levels have been found in the southwest, but levels well above average have been found in some other parts of England and parts of Scotland, Wales and Northern Ireland. However, even in these areas most homes have low levels. Most people receive a larger radiation dose from radon indoors than from any other source, including from the many industrial uses of radiation, nuclear power and medical exposures.

7 Can radon get into water supplies?

Yes, it could. Most water supplies have low levels of radon, but some smaller supplies may have high levels. None has been found in the UK with high enough levels to cause as much concern as radon from the ground. The Health Protection Agency endorses a proposed European guideline suggesting action if radon levels in private water supplies exceed 1,000 becquerels per litre.

9   Why systems fail

1 Why should we be so interested in the human factors at work?

The fact is that human error really is the ultimate cause of most accidents at work in some way or another. It is very rare that errors are deliberate, but people can make errors due to a lack of training, through poor design of equipment or machinery, or maybe just through the poor culture inherent within an organization. We must now manage that variable that is so difficult to manage that affects human behaviour – the organization and the control of the individuals – as it plays such a large part in accidents at work.

It is not the machines or work equipment that cause accidents, but rather the people who put the policies, plans, procedures and systems in place.

2 How big a part does the human factor play in accidents?

You could say as much as 98 % (with the other 2 % due to 'Acts of God', in the legal terminology), as people are always involved in one way or another. From examining accounts of actual incidents, it is possible to identify common causes of human error and typical system deficiencies that have led to these errors. Every large-scale accident contains an element of human error.

3 Can you give an example of human error?

The nuclear accident at the Tokaimura processing plant in Japan in 1999 was a prime example of human error, as concluded by the

International Atomic Energy Agency. The workers at the complex made a simple but critical error, adding eight times the correct amount of liquid uranium into a container of nitric acid. The intense heat of the resulting nuclear reaction caused a build-up of pressure inside the container, which exploded sending radioactive gas gushing into the atmosphere. The building in which the accident took place was not designed to contain radiation, and three nearby workers received massive doses of radiation, two of them fatal.

4 Surely the emphasis on physical and engineering controls will help reduce accidents?

Oh yes, absolutely! However, studies show that technical developments alone will not eliminate accidents at work. Emphasis should be placed on how people fit into and interact with their working environment.

5 Are there any key areas that we should be looking at?

According to the Health and Safety Executive, the factors relating to accidents and risk management that organizations should be looking at are:

- **job function**: this could be workload, suitability of work environment (e.g. free from disturbances or interruptions), maintenance of work equipment;
- **individual factors**: these encompass the attitude, motivation, perception and mental and physical state of staff, and can be influenced. The actions of individuals in an organization can impact on safety on a large scale;
- **organizational factors**: this could include work planning, health and safety management and the health and safety culture.

6 Is it not just a case of getting people to take more care?

No, the human element must be carefully managed, as human failure can be immediate or delayed. For example, active failures can have immediate consequences and are usually made by front line people such as operators, control room staff and drivers. But there can also be latent failures, which are decisions that are made by management. Latent failures could be failures in health and safety management systems, or poor design of plant and equipment, or even ineffective communications. These are examples of management failures.

7 Can you explain in more detail human error?

Human error can be defined as a decision that was not intended, and which involved a deviation from an accepted standard that led to an undesirable outcome. These errors often occur when stressors are present, such as a poor workplace environment or exceptional task demands. The errors fall into three categories: slips, lapses and mistakes. A slip is a failure to correctly carry out the actions of a task; a lapse is forgetting to carry out a task. Slips and lapses usually occur during routine or repetitive tasks requiring little attention: an example of a slip could be a machine operator inputting the wrong data on a keypad. This sort of thing can happen with very experienced people, such as maintenance operators. A lapse could be someone forgetting to perform a task due to an interruption, such as a maintenance man forgetting to isolate a machine.

Mistakes are a more complex type of human error where someone does the wrong thing when they believe that it is the right thing to do! For example, someone could attempt to remove the lid of a drum containing flammable liquid using a gas cutting torch, causing the drum to explode. This could be through a lack of knowledge, understanding or failure to communicate.

8 What are human violations?

A human violation is where someone knowingly breaks the rules at work. This could be, for example, someone removing a guard on a machine: an action that would clearly increase the risk to users' health and safety. However, these rules are broken for different reasons, often including a genuine desire to carry out a job to meet a production target. Violations are very rarely acts of sabotage or vandalism. Violations are divided into three categories: **routine**, **situational**, and **exceptional**.

A **routine violation** can occur when someone believes that the rules no longer apply: e.g. staff no longer wearing ear defenders. This could be the result of a poor health and safety culture at work.

To reduce the likelihood of this happening management need to increase training, improve communication and explain the reasons for wearing the ear defenders: i.e. to reduce the chances of occupational deafness.

A **situational violation** could be someone breaking the rules to meet production targets that might be unfairly set. The person breaking the rules may be under pressure, and management would need to encourage communication from staff when they feel under pressure and improve job design and planning with better supervision.

Exceptional violations, as the name suggests, happen very rarely and usually during an emergency situation. For example, a doctor might feel that the benefit outweighs the risks by ignoring a fire alarm and carrying on working on a patient as the hospital is being evacuated. Better training on emergency situations is needed in this case. In general, management should send out positive messages about health and safety rules by not breaking them – in other words, lead by example.

9 Do biological factors play a key part in human errors?

Our bodies do have physical limits that we cannot ignore, and we should consider that in the workplace. As we grow older we might become more experienced and aware of the dangers that we face; however, with old age comes a number of limiting factors that can affect performance. For example, eyesight, hearing and physical strength all deteriorate as we grow older. As the retirement age is pushed up the demographics of the workforce are changing accordingly, and designers of equipment need to consider that.

Another factor to consider, unrelated to age, is the possibility of eye impairments or 'colour blindness' among employees. Around 7 % of the population have defects in colour vision, and unfortunately this usually manifests as an inability to distinguish between red and green – the two colours used in most warning systems! To combat this, a designer may incorporate shapes as well as colour into their warning and indicator lamps. Other alternatives include audible warnings, where an immediate response is required. Studies have shown that where there is a combination of audible and visual warnings on machinery then there is a notable improvement in safety performance.

10 The costs of non-compliance

1 What effect does poor safety performance have?

Firstly, it indicates to employees and others – including inspectors – that the company is not 'people centred'. This can lead to low staff morale and, as a consequence, reduced productivity.

Secondly, the lack of a safety culture has an adverse effect on the profitability of a company. This was recently highlighted by a sudden collapse in a public limited company's share price due to the lack of health and safety standards, and the knock-on effect in terms of loss of reputation, credibility and customers.

Quite simply, by reducing accident-related costs you will reduce the overall cost base of the business and boost the underlying net profits. It is essential to recognize the extent of consequential losses and what could be termed 'hidden costs'.

2 Can you give a typical example of the consequences of poor safety performance?

If someone is injured then this could result in both a claim for damages and a criminal prosecution. Both of these suits will require a hefty amount of cash to defend, in addition to any pay settlements. If the cost of defending a case is, say, £4,000 then this must be paid out of the company profits.

For a company with net profits of 5 % of turnover (typical of a successful small to medium sized organization), then the turnover (or revenue from goods or services) that has to be generated to produce this amount of profit would be £80,000. This is the type of calculation that an accountant would use in evaluating the full cost of an incident at work.

So, if the company retails training shoes at £50 per pair, they would need to sell 1,600 units just to break even on those legal costs!

3 So a poor level of risk management sounds like giving away something for nothing?

Yes, that is exactly what it is like: this sort of cold analysis is what is needed to drum home the message in boardrooms around the UK.

When you talk to a managing director, the reduction in organizational costs thanks to their risk management policy is unlikely to be their first topic of conversation – but they could achieve a significant saving if they are willing to put in the time and money. A sound policy, rigorously implemented, could reward the director – and other interested parties – with a cracking return on investment.

4 What other 'interested parties'?

Internal parties such as employees, managers and sub-contractors will benefit directly from a sound risk management policy, but such a policy will also inspire confidence and bolster the organization's standing with external parties such as insurance companies, banks, venture capitalists and shareholders. In contrast, if your business has a poor health and safety record then just try raising some money, either from the banks or your shareholders!

5 Do you have any real-life examples of the costs of failing to implement a good risk management policy?

The Health and Safety Executive website describes several illuminating cases. For example, an injury to a worker using an unguarded machine cost a small fabrication company £45,000. The managing director was also prosecuted, and two employees had to be made redundant to keep the company afloat.

At the other end of the scale, a cheese manufacturer implemented a major initiative to tackle health and safety across its 10 sites. This helped to reduce accidents by 40 %, against an increase in productivity of 25 %.

Accidents in construction sites can cost around 6 % of the total project costs, and that is quite staggering!

6 What about the costs to smaller organizations?

Poor risk management could easily cause some smaller organizations to go out of business, as losing skilled workers, even for a few days, can have a bigger effect than direct financial costs might suggest. Many smaller organizations have little cushion against accidental losses and don't have any contingency or disaster recovery plans in place. A serious accident could put them out of business. According to the Health and Safety Executive, 60% of companies experiencing a disruption lasting more than nine days go out of business.

In addition, over half of all people that are injured at work are off work for more than one day, and nearly a quarter will be off for more than one week.

7 Are there implications for organizations with more than one business location?

Yes: a risk management policy needs to be implemented across all of an organization's sites of work. Very recently a concrete making company had their two directors imprisoned for manslaughter, charged under Section 2 and Section 37 of the Health and Safety at Work etc. Act 1974. The company were ordered to pay costs of £89,000 and fines totalling £75,000. Initially this was for an accident at one site, but following inspections at all of the company's other 13 sites they were found to have 'virtually non-existent safety standards' and were served with 15 enforcement and prohibition notices. These related to work at height, transport safety, locking-off machinery, use of hydrochloric acid, and the welfare of the workers – all of which were potentially life-threatening situations.

8 Is there help out there for all of this risk reduction stuff?

Many organizations will work with you to achieve compliance with your legal requirements, as well as provide guidance on introducing a cost-effective investment plan to reduce your health and safety costs with an acceptable return on investment.

The following sources of information may be useful.

- Barbour Index
  www.barbour-index.co.uk
- The British Standards Institution
  www.bsi-global.com
- The British Safety Council
  www.britishsafetycouncil.co.uk
- Health and Safety Executive, *Successful Health and Safety Management* (HSG 65)
  www.hse.gov.uk/pubns/books/hsg65.htm
- Institution of Occupational Safety and Health
  www.iosh.co.uk
- The International Labour Organization
  www.ilo.org
- The Institute of Risk Management
  www.theirm.org

Case study

A company was prosecuted for a health and safety accident in which an employee sustained a severe fracture to his lower left arm, after placing it in an unguarded machine to clear a blockage. The machine had a fixed guard which had been removed previously due to the need to clear blockages during shifts. Operatives tended to unblock the machine without properly isolating it, and they had no safe system of work.

The accident was avoidable and the machine should have had the correct safeguards in place.

The company was fined £4,000 and had to pay costs of £6,500 after admitting breaches of the Health and Safety at Work etc. Act 1974. In addition, the company's director received a £2,000 fine and was ordered to pay £3,250 in costs after pleading guilty to charges under the same legislation.

However, the financial costs to the company of not implementing a risk management policy would most likely go far beyond the penalties imposed by the courts. For example, there would be the costs of remedial work, likely loss of business reputation and work force morale, and a potential civil claim that the company would need to defend against. The final costs could be close to the six-figure mark than the sums mentioned above. Of course, while the costs of non-compliance can be high in financial terms, the injury to the employee can be for life.

Following the case, the company had to provide adequate instruction and training for all operators of similar equipment – this is particularly important for inexperienced operators. Dangerous parts of machinery must also be guarded, as stipulated under Regulation 11 of The Provision and Use of Work Equipment Regulations 1998. In addition to a new interlocked guard, a safe system of work was also introduced for clearing blockages, i.e. by proper isolation, lock-off and tag-off, rather than relying on accessing dangerous moving parts with a power source present.

Bibliography

EU legislation

The Treaty of Rome (1957)

The Low Voltage Directive (73/23/EEC)

The Use of Work Equipment Directive (89/655/EEC)

The Machinery Directive (98/37/EC and 2006/42/EC)

The Electromagnetic Compatibility Directive (2004/108/EC)

UK legislation

The Factory Health and Morals Act 1802

The Health and Safety at Work etc. Act 1974 (Chapter 37)

The Workplace (Health, Safety and Welfare) Regulations 1992 (SI 1992 no. 3004)

The Electrical Equipment (Safety) Regulations 1994 (SI 1994 no. 3260)

The Lifting Operations and Lifting Equipment Regulations 1998 (SI 1998 no. 2307)

The Provision and Use of Work Equipment Regulations 1998 (SI 1998 no. 2306)

The Management of Health and Safety at Work Regulations 1999 (SI 1999 no. 3242)

The Electromagnetic Compatibility Regulations 2006 (SI 2006 no. 3418)

The Construction (Design and Management) Regulations 2007 (SI 2007 no. 320)

The Corporate Manslaughter and Corporate Homicide Act 2007 (Chapter 19)

The Health and Safety (Offences) Act 2008 (Chapter 20)

The Supply of Machinery (Safety) Regulations 2008 (SI 2008 no. 1597)

Standards

BS 7121-1:2006, *Code of practice for safe use of cranes – General*

BS EN 13557, *Cranes – Controls and control stations*

BS EN 474-1:2006, *Earth-moving machinery – Safety – General requirements*

PD IEC/TR 61508-0:2005, *Functional safety of electrical/electronic/ programmable electronic safety-related systems – Functional safety and IEC 61508*

BS EN 692, *Machine tools – Mechanical presses – Safety*

BS OHSAS 18001:2007, *Occupational health and safety management systems – Requirements*

BS EN ISO 12100, *Safety of machinery – Basic concepts, general principles for design*

BS EN 60204-1:2006, *Safety of machinery – Electrical equipment of machines – General requirements*

BS EN 60204-32:2008, *Safety of machinery – Electrical equipment of machines – Requirements for hoisting machines*

BS EN 62061, *Safety of machinery – Functional safety of safety-related electrical, electronic and programmable electronic control systems*

BS EN 953:1997, *Safety of machinery – Guards – General requirements for the design and construction of fixed and movable guards*

BS EN 1088:1995, *Safety of machinery – Interlocking devices associated with guards – Principles for design and selection*

BS EN ISO 14121-1:2007, *Safety of machinery – Risk assessment – Principles*

BS EN 414, *Safety of machinery – Rules for the drafting and presentation of safety standards*

BS EN 954-1:1997, *Safety of machinery – Safety related parts of control systems – Part 1: General principles for design*

BS EN ISO 13849-1:2008, *Safety of machinery – Safety-related parts of control systems – General principles for design*

BS EN ISO 13849-2, *Safety of machinery – Safety-related parts of control systems – Validation*

Publications

HSE Information sheet MISC156

Index of questions by topic

BS EN ISO 13849-1, what standard should a machine builder use? (7:7, p74)

BS EN ISO 13849-1, is it just a case of selecting performance levels in this standard? (7:8, p75)

BS EN ISO 13849-1, can we comply by using either this or BS EN 954-1? (7:9, p75)

CE mark, does CE + CE = CE? (4:24, p52)

CE marking, is it a guarantee of safety? (4:13, p44)

Civil action, what are the consequences to an organization if an employee wins a claim against them? (3:19, p27)

Civil law and criminal law, what is the difference? (3:8, p20)

Common law, can you explain a bit about it? (3:7, p19)

'Conduct of their undertaking', what is meant by this? (3:2, p17)

Corporate risk management, what is this? (1:1, p1)

Declaration of conformity, what should it have on it? (4:20, p48)

Declaration of incorporation, when is this appropriate rather than a declaration of conformity? (4:21, p48)

Employers' liability insurance, what if the employer doesn't have it? (3:10, p21)

Employers' liability insurance certificates, should you keep previous certificates? (3:9, p21)

European Union, how much of an influence is it on UK legislation? (3:6, p19)

Harmonized standards, what is the background to these? (6:1, p63)

Harmonized standards, what benefits do they offer? (6:2, p63)

Hazardous substances, what are the physical properties of these? (8:4, p78)

Hazards, what are the biggest hazards? (8:2, p77)

Health and safety at work, what is it all about? (3:1, p17)

Health and Safety at Work etc. Act 1974, what are the relevant requirements of Section 6? (4:9, p41)

Health and safety inspectors, what powers do they have? (3:21, p29)

Health and safety inspectors, have they any additional powers? (3:25, p31)

Health and safety law, what am I responsible for as an employer? (3:11, p22)

Health and safety legislation, is it all fairly new and complicated? (3:3, p18)

Health and safety legislation, is it just the employers that have duties? (3:4, p18)

Health and safety legislation, who enforces this in the UK? (3:20, p28)

Health and safety notices, what if a company fails to comply with them? (3:22, p30)

Health and safety notices, what is the appeal process? (3:23, p30)

Health and safety policy, what is it and do we really need one? (3:15, p25)

Health and safety policy, what if we don't have one? (3:16, p25)

Health and safety, can you briefly describe its rise? (3:5, p18)

Health and safety, who has ultimate responsibility in an organization? (3:12, p23)

Health and safety, what are the directors' duties? (3:13, p24)

High-risk work environment, what is this? (8:1, p77)

High-risk work environment, how do you go about assessing one? (8:5, p79)

Human error, can you give a classic example? (9:3, p81)

Human error, can you explain it in more detail? (9:7, p83)

Human error, do biological factors play a key part? (9:9, p85)

Human factors, why should we be so interested in these at work? (9:1, p81)

Human violations, what are these? (9:8, p84)

Improvement notice, can it be extended? (3:24, p31)

Insurance, how does an insurance company work out the cost? (2:7, p12)

Insurance brokers, why do they charge a fee when they already receive commission from the insurer? (2:4, p11)

Insurance manager, what is the difference between this and a risk manager? (2:3, p10)

Machinery Directive, can you give me some background information? (4:1, p35)

Machinery Directive, does it apply to all EU countries? (4:3, p36)

Machinery, does new machinery have to be made to conform to any particular standards? (4:12, p43)

Machinery, what if it is manufactured by someone else either in the UK or elsewhere in the EEA and I (as a supplier) consider that the safeguards or other protective devices are inadequate? (4:14, p44)

Machinery, what language is acceptable for the instructions for the machinery? (4:17, p47)

Machinery, when will it be issued with a declaration of conformity? (4:19, p47)

'Negligence', what does it mean in the context of risk management? (2:8, p13)

Negligence, what is it? (3:17, p25)

Negligence claim, how can an employer defend a claim? (3:18, p26)

Notified body, is it mandatory to use a notified body for testing? (4:23, p51)

Professional indemnity insurance policy, what does it cover? (2:5, p11)

Professional indemnity insurance policy, will it cover an organization for the actions of consultants, sub-contractors or agents who provide advice or services on their behalf? (2:6, p12)

Provision and Use of Work Equipment Regulations 1998, what is the background to these? (5:1, p55)

Provision and Use of Work Equipment Regulations 1998, what equipment is covered by the regulations? (5:2, p56)

Provision and Use of Work Equipment Regulations 1998, who do the regulations apply to? (5:3, p56)

Provision and Use of Work Equipment Regulations 1998, what do the regulations require me to do? (5:4, p57)

Provision and Use of Work Equipment Regulations 1998, how do the regulations compare and relate to other health and safety legislation? (5:5, p60)

Provision and Use of Work Equipment Regulations 1998, how do employees ensure the safe use of work equipment or machinery? (5:6, p60)

Radioactivity, what are the risks from radioactivity in the workplace? (8:6, p79)

Radon, can it get into water supplies? (8:7, p80)

Risk management, what could it do for my business? (1:2, p1)

Risk management, can I guarantee success by implementing it? (1:5, p2)

Risk management, what is meant by 'dynamic'? (1:10, p5)

Risk management, is there an explicit requirement in legislation to implement it? (1:11, p6)

Risk management, what is the role of insurance? (2:1, p9)

Risk management, so a poor level of risk management sounds like giving away something for nothing? (10:3, p88)

Risk management, who are the 'interested parties'? (10:4, p88)

Risk management, do you have any real-life examples of the costs of failing to implement a good risk management policy? (10:5, p88)

Risk management, what about the costs to smaller organizations? (10:6, p89)

Risk management, are there implications for organizations with more than one business location? (10:7, p89)

Risk management, is there help out there for all of this cost reduction stuff? (10:8, p90)

Risk management policy, should we have one as well a safety policy? (1:9, p5)

Risk management system, what is this? (1:3, p1)

Risk management system, what are the consequences of not implementing one? (1:4, p1)

Risk manager, should I employ one? (1:8, p4)

Risk managers, do they attend to the company's insurance needs? (2:2, p9)

Safety performance, what is the effect of poor performance? (10:1, p87)

Safety performance, can you give a typical example of the consequences of poor safety performance? (10:2, p87)

Standards, why do they always have different prefixes? (6:3, p64)

Standards, what are some of the key machinery safety standards? (6:4, p64)

Standards, can you give a brief overview on the classification of the machinery safety standards, as it seems complex? (6:5, p66)

Standards, can you tell us a bit more about those C standards? (6:6, p67)

Technical file, what is it, and what should be included in it? (4:15, p45)

Technical file, where can it be kept? (4:18, p47)

Terminology, is there some that we need to understand? (1:7, p3)

Toxic, what does this mean? (8:3, p78)

Training, what sort of training would an enforcement officer expect my company to undertake? (5:7, p61)